# FINDING COMMON GROUND

*Mental Illness Recognition and
Crisis Response for Law Enforcement*

RICHARD CRINO

ISBN: 978-1-4834-1023-4 (sc)
ISBN: 978-1-4834-1024-1 (e)

Front cover photographed by Detective Sgt. Kevin Sanford
of the Woonsocket Police Department.

Lulu Publishing Services rev. date: 03/16/2015

# CONTENTS

# ACKNOWLEDGMENTS

I would like to give special thanks to the men and women of law enforcement who shared both their work experiences and expertise in helping me understand the law enforcement perspective in responding to emotionally disturbed suspects. I would like to especially thank retired police lieutenant Robin Winslow, who worked with me on the design and facilitation of the Certified Crisis Response training (CCRT) for law enforcement mentioned throughout this book. Special thanks to Rhode Island CCRT graduates, Officer Richard Parenti from the Scituate PD, Sgt. Mike Villiard from the Woonsocket PD, Officer Sandra Marinucci, and Sgt. Roland Coutu from the West Warwick PD, and Police Chief Rick Ramsey from the West Greenwich PD. I would also like to thank Kim Micucci, BA, LCDP from NRI Community Services who helped co-facilitate many of the trainings. Their skill, dedication, and understanding of the issues regarding this topic is both admired and appreciated.

# FOREWORD

My colleagues and I were asked to write the following editorial in response to an editorial which appeared in the Providence Journal following the Washington, D.C. naval shipyard shooting in 2013. The editorial mis-stated that police officers in the state of Rhode Island were not adequately trained in handling mentally ill individuals in crisis. The following editorial was written to "set the record straight", and highlight the success and continued efforts of both law enforcement and mental health providers in Rhode Island to address this very important issue.

## Mental Illness and Law Enforcement

Date: November 1, 2013, *Providence Journal*

The need to assess the mental status and intentions of individuals has become a routine requirement of police officers performing enforcement and investigation functions. More often than not, they are the first responders when situations arise in the community. Their police academy training fosters a response that emphasizes arrest and control.

The understanding, however, that the law enforcement community must respond differently to persons with behavioral health diagnoses is becoming more widespread. The more typical and traditional police response often results in injuries, escalation in crisis behavior, and public incidents. In the case of persons diagnosed with behavioral health issues, it is critical that police officers are able to recognize when they encounter someone with these issues and that the officers have the skills necessary to balance their personal and public safety concerns with the safety and care of the person with the mental illness.

The Certified Crisis Responder Program (CCRT) was designed in Rhode Island to respond to both public and law enforcement concerns regarding the lack of de-escalation and crisis response training offered to police officers statewide. NRI Community Services, Inc. has provided smaller scale law enforcement training since 1999. NRICS partnered with police representatives and state officials from various local departments to co design Rhode Island's first crisis intervention certification program for police. For several years the Rhode Island Council of Community Mental Health Organizations has had a training contract from the Rhode Island Division of Behavioral Healthcare. This contract has made CCRT training available to RI police departments at no cost. Officers who attend the RI four-day CCRT training program receive specialized training that includes the following: crisis intervention techniques, mental illness signs and symptoms, police use of less lethal options, excited delirium, and drug-induced crisis management. There is a full day of crisis role-playing in which officer's test and practice learned techniques in real-life role-play scenarios. Officers interested in becoming trainers also receive instruction on how to present this information to their peers. The "train the trainers" portion of this initiative includes three to four practice sessions by the officer within his or her department, with feedback from a mental health professional. Trained officers (in partnership with NRICS) also provide three to four hours of mental illness training to police departments when requested. To achieve certification, officers are required to pass a written exam, perform well in role-play scenarios, and have an additional twenty hours of training in related topics.

The results of the program are impressive! Officers who have attended the four-day CCRT as well as those officers who have attended the four-hour department-level trainings are reporting very positive outcomes in the field. Learned techniques are being applied with great success. In one case, an officer used the learned techniques to safely assist a client with schizophrenia who was walking into the middle of a busy intersection with a shopping cart. The officer guided the individual out of traffic by using verbal techniques, allowed the individual to smoke one cigarette, and after a short exchange was able to walk the individual into a waiting ambulance. The officer turned to his sergeant, who was a CCRT officer, and stated, "Sarge, this shit really works!"

The Certified Crisis Responder Program, while successfully training officers in crisis techniques, has also produced many excellent police trainers in Rhode Island. The undersigned assure the ongoing success of this program by volunteering countless hours to assist their fellow officers in understanding this very important training topic. The total amount of officers that have completed the four-day CCRT training stands at one hundred and four. Of this number, forty-one officers have gone on to become certified as CCRT trainers. Additionally, in just the past six months, 180 police officers and/or new recruits have benefited from receiving three to four department-level mental health trainings as part of this initiative.

Community mental health centers (CMHCs), police department training officers, and the police academies provide information and techniques to hundreds of police officers annually.

The CCRT effort in Rhode Island is having a very positive effect on CMHC and police department collaboration. Mental health and law enforcement are moving in the right direction in intervening with mentally ill adults. Changing the current mental health laws in Rhode Island does not seem to be needed, as some letter writers have advocated.

Please consider advocating for state support to all cities and towns for police training and mental health collaboration. Building these relationships and skills should not be based on the type of community served, the police department's accreditation status, or the size of the police department's training budget. Nor should these trainings be interrupted by changes in police chiefs, training officers, or key staff at community mental health centers.

*Forward contributors included Richard Crino, vice president of acute services at NRI Community Services; Christian Stephens, president and CEO of NRI Community Services, Barbara Inderlin, LICSW; and four of the CCRT trainers: Officer Richard Dean Parenti of Scituate Police, Chief Richard N. Ramsay of West Greenwich Police, Sgt. Mike Villiard of Woonsocket Police, and Robin Winslow, retired police lieutenant and professor of criminal justice at New England Technical Institute.*

For more information about the CCRT program, contact Richard Crino, RN, vice president of acute services at NRI Community Services. Mr. Crino can be reached at 401-235-7000, or by email @ rncrino@verizon.net

# INTRODUCTION

Law enforcement officers come in contact with individuals experiencing a mental health crisis every day while they are performing their duties. Whether it is an individual on the street throwing a brick through a window or an inmate requiring restraint for suicidal actions, officers are frequently involved in challenging and at times dangerous situations involving people in crisis.

As a registered nurse specializing in mental health and law enforcement consultation for the past thirty years, I've spent a good amount of my time training police and correction officers in how to recognize and respond to individuals experiencing a mental health crisis. I decided to specialize in this area after looking at the lack of training information on mental illness provided by many police and correction organizations nationwide. This made little sense to me as interacting with the public and crisis management is a daily expectation of the job. While I began providing this training on my own, I eventually partnered up with a police training officer, Lt. Robin Winslow. Lt. Winslow's law enforcement background and experience helped shape the training program into an effective, hands-on, and realistic training experience for the officers in attendance. The training certification program is called the Certified Crisis Responder Trainer Program or CCRT. Oftentimes I co-train with veteran law enforcement officers who successfully completed the CCRT Program. The following chapters will include much of the didactic and hands-on components of this training program.

Most law enforcement officers learn early that making quick and accurate decisions is critical for survival. Another important survival skill is maintaining a balance approach when dealing with someone in crisis. This can be achieved by not overreacting to situations, such as going hands-on to fast, or underreacting by letting their guard down. What many officers may not be aware of is that relying on their training and natural instincts will not only keep them safe but also make them good communicators on the job. In fact, some of the officers I work with are as good as or better than mental health professionals when it comes to de-escalating someone in crisis.

Remember, I am not trying to turn law enforcement officers into social workers. I will not tell officers that part of their job is to diagnose or treat individuals they come in contact with. Nor will I expect officers to compromise officer safety for establishing rapport with an individual in crisis. Rather, the information in this book is designed to help officers develop a better understanding of mental illness, differentiate between criminally motivated behaviors and behaviors of a person experiencing mental illness (non-criminal intent), and to improve verbal communication during crisis situations.

Another premise of this book is to help officers strengthen their empathy for the mentally ill population. I define empathy as the ability to "walk in the shoes" of another human being. Remember, mental illness can strike anyone, including you or your immediate family members. In explaining empathy further to officers in attendance at my seminars, I often pose the following question: "If your brother, sister, or parent was experiencing an emotional crisis in a neighboring community, how would you want the responding officers to treat them?"

The National Institute of Mental Health in a recent survey reported that 26 percent of American adults have a diagnosable mental illness. A 2004 Department of Justice survey of federal and state prison populations found that the highest percentages of mentally ill inmates were incarcerated in local jails. The report cited 64.2 percent of inmates in local jails as either having been issued a clinical diagnosis of mental illness or having received treatment by a mental health professional. Simply put, there are a lot of folks out there struggling with mental health issues, and the chances of you facing them in the community or cell block when they are in emotional crisis is an everyday reality!

*Finding Common Ground* is designed to help law enforcement officers improve their knowledge and skill in the following areas:

+ how to distinguish between criminal and noncriminal behaviors
+ how to effectively deal with suicidal individuals
+ how to effectively deal with individuals who are hallucinating or experiencing delusional thoughts
+ how to deal with intoxicated suspects
+ how to determine whether an individual is a danger to self or others
+ how to understand the mental health law
+ how to effectively gain compliance with mentally ill individuals in crisis
+ how to use nonlethal options during street encounters
+ how to deal with an excited delirium suspect

The information, techniques, and strategies presented in the following pages are based on actual "in the field" experience. While no technique is guaranteed to work 100 percent of the time, you will find this information highly useful in performing your duties.

# CHAPTER 1

# CRISIS INTERVENTION

Law enforcement officers are oftentimes called upon to assist in noncriminal or nonviolent incidents involving people in crisis. A crisis can develop when a person's normal ways of dealing with stress have not worked or have broken down. A crisis is usually short-lived and ends with a resolution that could be positive or negative, good or bad. A crisis feels crushing to the person, leaving him or her unable to cope or to adjust to the situation. Often the person in crisis doesn't believe the crisis will end. A crisis can be caused when a person experiences a loss of a loved one, a job, income, or a home or when the person suffers an accident, a crime, a divorce, or a separation just to name a few. Without help, the person is left feeling helpless. The individual simply does not know what to do to control the situation. In short, a crisis can psychologically paralyze us.

When a person in crisis is not handling or responding well to stressor, crisis intervention is used to help the person solve the crisis and hopefully learn better ways to deal with stress in the future. A person in a crisis usually has feelings of anxiety, helplessness, fear, inadequacy, confusion, agitation, and disorganization.

The primary goal in a crisis is to identify, assess, and intervene; to return the person to his or her prior level of functioning as quickly as possible; and to lessen any negative impact on the parties involved.

1

Sometimes during this process new skills and coping mechanisms are gained, resulting in change. We are not talking here about an individual who is actively committing a crime or fleeing a crime scene or committing a violent act against another person. This is an individual who needs support, reassurance, and guidance to safety.

Good communication with the person experiencing a crisis is crucial. The more disorganized the person is, the more organized an officer will need to be. It is also important to help all individuals experiencing a crisis regain focus. An officer can accomplish this by both asking the individual to focus on their voice and by repeating supportive statements. Once the officer makes contact, it is important to reassure the individual that he or she is safe and that the officer is there to help. It's also important to give the person time to express thoughts and concerns. In fact, you'd rather have the details come out at a pace that is controlled as opposed to a rapid emotional release, which could be overwhelming for the person. Let the person tell you his or her story in as much detail as he or she can handle. As long as the person is not threatening, aggressive, or presenting a danger to themselves, others, or the officers on scene, time is on the side of the officer. Officers also need to remain calm in voice tone and volume. Raising one's voice (without anger) is okay as long as it occurs in an effort to gain the person's attention. While an assessment of a person in crisis usually begins with an evaluation of what he or she says, physical movements, facial expressions, posture, and mannerisms, are also important. Remember, assessing intent and dangerousness of the individual still needs is the top priority for law enforcement officers responding to a crisis.

The good news is that officers can effectively establish trust, provide orientation, offer hope and reassurance; and provide leadership to individuals in crisis by applying simple, easy-to-learn, common sense verbal techniques.

The first crisis scenario we will discuss will involve what is known as a critical incident event. Auto accidents, natural disasters, terrorist attacks, and victimization by physical or sexual assault are examples of critical incident events. In this type of crisis situation, an officer's help is most often welcomed as opposed to those involving criminal or potentially violent situations where officers are not greeted with open arms.

To illustrate, let's take the example of an officer providing assistance at the scene of an auto accident. One evening officer Johnson, a 5 year veteran of the force, receives a call from dispatch with instructions to respond to an auto accident involving a young woman. When the officer arrived, he/she noticed that there was a woman at the side of the road in tears. The woman's car apparently struck a road sign and veered off the road and landed in a ditch. On approaching the women officer Johnson quickly determined that the women appeared in distress with no outword signs of aggression or criminal intent. The officer then proceded to assess the woman's physical/medical condition to determine if first aid was needed prior to medical personnel arriving on scene. When providing crisis intervention, assessing the need for medical care should be a top priority once safety has been assessed. Being current in first aid and CPR skills is a must for law enforcement officers as most often the police arrive on scene before medical personnel. In getting back to the senerio, the officer's assessment should begin by assessing with the A, B, and C's of first aid which are airway, breathing, and circulation. While most nonmedical personnel, including law enforcement officers, are hopeful that first aid won't be needed before rescue or medical personnel arrives, many times it does. If the woman did not appear to be breathing (no chest movement), beginning rescue breathing as per CPR protocols, would be appropriate. The chest compressions of CPR should also be initiated if no pulse is detected. If the woman presented unconscious or severely injured, the officer could also use verbal techniques to assist until medical personnel arrive on scene. Words of encouragement would also be appropriate for the responding officer to use when applying first aid, whether the woman presented conscious or not. If she presented unconscious or severely injured (unable to speak and on the ground), words of encouragement and support could be delivered by the officer by kneeling to the ground and speaking into the women's ear. Even though the woman presents unconscious, she may still have the ability to comprehend words. There are numerous cases of people who were unconscious at an accident scene that could accurately recall sounds around them, even though they were not conscious during the event. Officer Johnson may also be the last person the woman see's or hear's from before her death, so continuing to communicate is a must! The words spoken by the officer at the scene could also help the women feel a sense of company, helping to reduce her fear and anxiety. So whether an individual presents alert or unconscious at a crisis scene, the same approach and verbal techniques apply. If the woman were bleeding from an open wound, applying pressure while using verbal skills would also be effective.

When I was a young medic in the US Army, I was taught to have injured soldiers participate in their own healing to assist in their recovery. For example, when I was applying first aid to a soldier for a lacerated wound, I would often have the injured soldier apply pressure to the wound and/or assist in the wound-cleaning process by holding bandages, applying antiseptic, etc. Another technique in treating a lacerated/ bleeding wound is to ask the injured person to close their eyes and focus on making their own blood clot to seal the wound. The human brain and body controls the release of blood-clotting factors, so using one's thoughts to start the clotting process is possible! These techniques are surprisingly effective in helping people actively participate in their own recovery, thus promoting the physical and psychological healing process. These techniques are also helpful in refocusing a person's attention away from the pain and anxiety that is common during medical trauma, restoring a sense of control over the situation. Remember, critical incidents such as auto accidents, shooting and assaults are unexpected and produce great feelings of helplessness in the injured person. The quicker traumatized individuals can be assisted in restoring a sense of control, the faster they can move to recovery. The good news is that the above techniques are just as effective for children and adolescents as they are for adults.

Getting back to our example, let's take a look at what communication techniques might be appropriate for the officer to use at the crisis scene. He or she could begin by approaching the woman, introducing him or her self, informing her of what happened and reassuring her she will be okay. This can be accomplished by using phrases such as: "Ma'am, my name is John, I'm a police officer, and I'm here to help." "What is your name?" "You have been involved in an accident." "Rescue is on the way." "You're going to be okay." "The worst part of the accident is over." "I will stay here with you (safety) until rescue arrives." If the woman begins hyperventilating or gasping for air, the officer can utilize deep breathing to enhance relaxation. This can be accomplished by having the woman refocus her thoughts on her breathing, which should reestablish both normal breathing and a relaxed state. A simple statement such as, "Ma'am I want you to breathe with me as this will help you relax", may be all that is needed. In applying this technique, the officer might ask the women if she would allow him to assist her with her breathing. Gaining approval before implementing assistance again allows the woman to play a role in her own healing. Once obtaining permission to help, the officer would then instruct the woman to breathe slowly in through her nose and then out through her mouth. This command would be repeated until the woman's breathing returned to normal. It's important to have the women exhale longer than the inhale to engage the body's natural relaxation response. This breathing exercise usually works well in reducing both anxiety and hyperventilating.

It may be helpful here to quickly review the power of breathing in reducing a person's stress level before we continue with our example. Why is it that law enforcement officers and soldiers are told to breathe during tactical training? Why is it that major league pitchers breathe before each pitch, and NBA players take a deep breath before taking free throws? It is because slow, deep breathing has been shown to lower a person's heart rate, improve focus and concentration; as well as lower the amount of stress hormones released into the body. Experts in the field of stress tell us that slow, deep breathing lowers heart rate and stress hormone release by turning on what is known as "the relaxation response". By activating the relaxation response a person can voluntarily turn down his or her nervous system, thus reducing anxiety. In our example, the responding officer could use this technique by having the woman close her eyes and slowly breathe in through her nose and out through her mouth. The officer could also instruct her to hold her breath for four seconds after inhaling, and then let the breath out through her mouth for six seconds. Exhaling longer than inhalation is the key; as it is the exhalation phase of breathing that engages the relaxation response. The officer could also add visualization to this breathing exercise by asking the women to picture herself in a relaxing environment such as a past vacation spot, beach house, being on a lake, etc., as she continue to breath. This technique called "visualization" helps lower stress levels by helping a person recall an enjoyable memory from their past eliciting a positive and relaxing response. While visualization can work well at a crisis scene, it can be practiced by everyone on a daily basis to lower stress levels and bring peace of mind.

During a crisis and/or traumatic event, in particular those events which are life threatening such as accidents, shootings, assaults, and disasters, most people experience what are known as "emotional aftershocks." These emotional aftershocks are normal manifestations of stress. There are five known categories of stress that individuals might experience after being involved in a crisis or traumatic event. Physical reactions of stress can be experienced as headaches, vomiting, shaking, and shortness of breath, nausea, and vomiting. Thinking reactions of stress can be manifested by memory loss, confusion, reoccurring thoughts of the event, and nightmares. Emotional reactions of stress may manifest as anxiety, sadness, fear, anger, and blame. Behavioral stress reactions can also occur, such as aggression, excess drinking (after the event), isolation, and engaging in risky behavior can also be seen. Spiritual stress can present as a person being angry with God. These reactions are normal and usually subside over time. It is also common for law enforcement officers to experience stress reactions at the scene of a critical incident event. Again, stress reactions are normal and expected to occur during frightening/stressful events.

One of the key's to providing effective crisis management, is to help people understand they are not going crazy and that the above stress reactions are normal and would be experienced by anyone placed in a similar situation. This technique helps normalize the experience.

Let's take a closer look at what experts in the field of stress believe may cause these stress aftershocks or reactions to occur. During a crisis event a person's fight-or-flight response is most often activated to help the person survive the event. The fight or flight response is the brain's way of communicating to us that we are in a dangerous situation and need to fight, flee or freeze. This response is analogous to a fire alarm going off during a fire. When activated, the fight or flight response triggers the release of stress hormones into a person's body to assist survival by increasing blood pressure, heart rate, and breathing. This is one reason we may see people with cardiovascular disease (high blood pressure, obesity, clogged arteries, etc.) experiencing heart attacks, strokes, and irregular heartbeats during a crisis. Stress hormones may also produce changes in a person's vision and hearing. As a way to protect a person from being overwhelmed by the experience, the human brain may inhibit the ability to hear what is being said. It is believed that stress hormones may also be responsible for producing changes in a person's vision, though this phenomenon is not wholly understood at this time. Vision changes may occur in a person's depth perception. Depth perception is the ability to tell how close or how far an object is to us. Stress hormones are also believed to be responsible for making a person vomit, involuntarily urinate or defecate; which again is a natural survival response designed to make an individual lighter and quicker to escape the situation. Time distortion is another common phenomenon that may occur. This is experienced as either time slowing down or speeding up. It's believed that time distortion occurs because of the effects of stress hormones on a section of the brain responsible for memory. This part of the brain tells us who we are, where we are, and what time of day it is. It also gives us the ability to put our thoughts into words. If this part of the brain shuts down, as may occur in traumatic events, people experience memory loss, confusion, and an inability to use words to explain what happened. Individuals involved in a traumatic event may also present confused, dazed, or in a panic state.

It is important to keep in mind that stress reactions could also be related to head trauma or other medical conditions sustained during the incident. This is why medical evaluation should not be overlooked for this population!

Again, the power of words in the healing process cannot be overstated. Trauma survivors oftentimes have strong memory for psychological support given at crisis scenes, such as having their hands held, being given blankets, or being carried to safety. It is also believed that psychological support given at a crisis scene may be more effective and longer lasting than help received at a later date, such as that provided by a crisis worker in the hospital setting. One explanation on why memory for support received in the immediate aftermath of a crisis may be stronger , is that the human brain may be more open to suggestion during the early stages of trauma. Helpful actions and words of encouragement from others may enhance the brain's ability to find a quick and effective solution to reduce both the physical and emotional discomfort experienced by the person. It is believed that during life-threatening experiences the brain may place in memory those aspects of the event, both good and bad, that have the strongest emotional impact. So while this could involve seeing shocking images and hearing upsetting sounds, positive occurrences involving comfort (food and blankets), encouragement ("I will help you get through this") and medical care (first aid) also have a strong impact on memory. It is also important to protect a person involved in a crisis from experiencing further physical or emotional harm. Leading them to safety, seeking immediate medical attention, and preventing them from seeing further traumatic images are examples of ways to reduce harm experienced during traumatic events.

Another important aspect of dealing with crisis situations is being prepared for the possibility of violence occuring. Police and correction officers routinely have to de-escalate potentially violent suspects. Several years back I was asked to design a training program for emergency room personnel on how to deal with aggressive patients. I based the design of the program on the principles of medical triage, which I learned during my medical training in the US Army. In disasters and mass-causality incidents, military and civilian emergency medical teams use a color-coded system to identify and treat medical casualties who are in need of treatment. Typically RNs, Medic's or MDs are located at the front entrance of the treatment sites, and their job is to direct casualties to the appropriate medical station based on the severities of the person's injuries. If the individual had severe, life-threatening problems with their airway, breathing, or circulation, or if they were in need of advanced medical care, they would be sent to an area color-coded red. If their issues were less severe but in need of hospital-level care, they would be moved to the area color-coded yellow. If their injuries were minor, they would be sent to the green area. So red, yellow, and green are the universal colors used for medical triage. This system ensures that medical resources are used appropriately and individuals are appropriately treated based on the severity of their injuries. Coincidently these happen to be the colors of a traffic light—red (critical), yellow (caution), and green (go). The violence prevention program outlined below utilizes this medical color-coding system to identify common problematic behaviors seen in individuals who are escalating to violence. I have used the medical triage analogy in the past when I have trained medical personnel. The stoplight analogy works well when I am training law enforcement and other nonmedical professionals. The concept is easy to learn and applies well in real-life situations.

## The Non-Violent Green Light Stage

Individuals in the green light stage are rarely violent. They are most often experiencing strong emotional reactions to significant stressors or are experiencing signs and symptoms of mental illness. The following behaviors can be seen during this stage:

+ showing signs of depression, sadness, and tearfulness

+ demonstrating increased energy, agitation, anxiety, pacing, and/or restlessness
+ verbally expressing frustration and anger
+ wringing of the hands and/or running hands through one's hair
+ looking confused or dazed
+ hearing voices or expressing false beliefs as seen in psychotic disorders

Remember, most individuals in the green light stage are in need of help and understanding. Officers can effectively maintain officer safety and convey both understanding and empathy to this population. Empathy again is the ability of a person to see a problem from another person's perspective. Walking in the shoes of another person can help officers avoid passing judgment to quickly or misunderstanding a person's communication. If officers intervene during this green stage, violence can oftentimes be prevented.

## The "Green Stage" Approach

It is important to keep in mind that maintaining a safe barrier between you and a person experiencing a mental health crisis is a must (three to five feet with hands in view). This is important for the safety of both parties involved. It is also important for officers to not close in on the individual too quickly, as this oftentimes exacerbates violence. For example, individuals who are fearful or experiencing paranoid thoughts need good spacing between themselves and others. While officer safety training dictates the importance of seeing the hands of all suspects, paranoid individuals also are concerned with seeing the hands of officers. Paranoid individuals oftentimes fear being assaulted or harmed by individuals with concealed weapons or objects. Officers can alleviate these fears by keeping their hands within view of the individual during these encounters. The following tips have also been found effective when one is approaching a person in the green stage of crisis:

+ Remain calm with a neutral tone. (Do not raise your voice.) Raising one's voice is appropriate when a person is not listening or hearing voices as the result of psychosis.
+ Encourage the person to be seated.
+ Be friendly to all.
+ Use first names when speaking.
+ Make good eye contact when communicating.
+ Listen before speaking.
+ Do not touch the individual unless there is a danger to self or others.
+ Show empathy and understanding. This can be achieved by listening to the individual's concerns and by letting the person know that his or her feelings are understandable given the situation.

An officer can also show understanding by using statements such as the following:

+ "If that happened to me, I'd be upset too."
+ "I can see how you would feel that way."
+ "You know... it's okay to feel like that."
+ "Lots of people in your position would feel the same way."

The previous phrases use the communication principles called normalization ("If that happened to me—"), summarization ("Let me see that I understand—"), and reflection ("You seem frustrated—").

Oftentimes when officers use these techniques, individuals report feeling understood and compassion from the responding officer. The old adage that it is not what you say but how you say it is true in many instances. Experts in the field tell us that communication is approximately 70 percent nonverbal and 30 percent verbal. Examples of nonverbal communication include facial expression, tone of voice, body posture, and eye contact. If you frown, check your watch, sigh, roll your eyes, clench your jaw, or speak in an angry tone, your words will have less meaning. This is probably where the phrase "kill them with kindness" comes from. A person in emotional crisis is most often looking for someone who will show both patience and understanding while listening to their side of the story. They are also looking for someone who will listen without passing judgment on their actions/situation.

Individuals in crisis also need someone to either guide them to safety or set limits on behaviors that are dangerous or inappropriate. The techniques used in the green light phase have a high success rate in preventing violence. An important point to emphasis is the importance of giving these situations time! Most individuals experiencing a mental health crisis need time to gather their thoughts and to trust that the officers are there to help and not harm them. The goal of green light interventions is to gain compliance by using the least amount of force possible. When individuals are not listening to what is being said to them, are refusing to comply with directives, and are becoming angry or aggressive, they are progressing to the "yellow light phrase."

# Verbal Aggressive/Threatening Stage Techniques (Yellow Light)

Behaviors that may indicate individuals are in the yellow light stage may include the following:

- The person does not cooperate with your suggestions.
- The person does not agree to sit down.
- The person demonstrates angry outbursts, such as yelling, hitting the desk, fist clenching, etc.
- The person makes verbal threats or insults.
- The person is speaking loudly, pointing fingers, or shaking fists.
- The person may be disrobing and/or taking off jewelry, hats, coats, etc.
- The person may be staring without blinking (which could be a indication of a possible impending attack). It is believed that the human brain may inhibit the blinking reflex in preparation for attack.

If the person is beginning to lose control and is making verbal threats to officers or others, it is important to set limits on his or her behaviors. If time and safety permit, giving the person choices may help in gaining compliance. While officers are in charge of directing the outcome, giving agitated individuals a say in the course of action gives them the impression that they control the outcome. This approach helps individuals regain control of their emotional states while also enhancing compliance. It also helps the individuals save face in front of friends, family, bystanders, or other inmates. Individuals who feel disrespected or embarrassed oftentimes lash out as a way to save face.

For example, consider the following statements: "You can sit down and stop yelling, or we will need to physically escort you out of the building." "John, which option do you want to do?" If the person becomes agitated, talks over you, make threats, or does not select an option, you should repeat the request again. If he or she still does not comply with your request, you will need to select the option for the individual. We are only talking about giving the person another sixty to ninety seconds or so after the second request for suspects who are not mentally ill. If you see that a mentally ill person is not complying because he or she does not understand your request, you may need to repeat it several more times until the individual does indeed understand your request. What I'm saying again is that giving a severely mentally ill person more time to follow your directive works better for all parties involved. The mentally person in crisis has trouble making decisions, and this "give it time" approach is used with good success. For example, a slight modification may be to state the above like this: "John, we are here to help and will not let people harm you or let you harm others." We want you to put the stick down and walk safely to with us." You would repeat this until the person complied, which may take up to twenty minutes! As long as they are not posing an imminent threat give the situation time. If the individual requests a cigarette, let him or her smoke. Smoking actually has an antianxiety effect on a person in crisis. "John, I will let you have a cigarette as long as you agree to walk to the rescue after finishing one smoke." So while it is okay to let the person smoke, you may need to keep the conversation going and keep reminding him or her of the agreement. A five-minute smoke is reasonable.

It is also important to try to get the person to sit down. "If you don't sit down, you will need to leave." The following tips are also helpful when you are dealing with individuals in the yellow stage:

- Call for backup as soon as possible.
- Do not tell them to calm down. It is better to say, "I need you to stop yelling at me. If you don't stop, you will need to leave."
- Do not argue with the person. Simply restate your request or remove the person from the area.

Reaching phrase yellow in a prison setting may be handled differently because of the unique circumstances found in a corrections environment. In preparation for writing this book and to get a better idea of how inmates are deescalated in crisis, I interviewed Jim Rathbun, a thirty-three-year veteran (retired) and former supervisor of correction officers' training at the adult corrections facility in Cranston, RI. The following information was obtained from my informative discussions with Mr. Rathbun.

It is not uncommon for correction officers to be significantly outnumbered by inmates. In the RI facility one correction officer may be responsible for up to a hundred inmates! While this ratio is reported by the RI facility, this one-officer-to-hundred-inmates ratio is most likely the norm here in the United States. This information is a bit scary since most correction officers are equipped with only radios and handcuffs. Lethal and less lethal options carried by police, such as firearms, batons, OC, and Tasers, are not carried by correction officers. The previous tactical options, which are necessary for police officers, pose a significant threat to the safety of correction officers if carried. Correction officers are at greater risk of being overtaken in a struggle because they are so heavily outnumbered. In correction facilities, less lethal options are available and can be brought to the scene depending on the severity of the situation. Having limited tactical options at the ready highlights the importance of correction officers having good verbal de-escalation skills. Phase yellow techniques for the aggressive and noncompliant inmate may begin differently than what is recommended for police. Being significantly outnumbered correction officers need to move hands-on a bit quicker than police. These interventions usually begin with an officer giving verbal commands for the inmates to lie facedown and to place their hands behind their backs. Once the inmates are secured and cuffed, they are placed in the closest cell until the officer is back in control. Rathbun did state that despite the rapid hands-on approach used by officers, training strongly emphasizes the use of verbal techniques throughout the restraint process. Verbal commands focus on orienting the inmate to current and future happenings. "We're carrying you to the nearest cell until you calm down." "You will stay in the cell until you agree to follow our commands." If the inmate is hallucinating, exhibiting suicidal tendencies, or expressing delusional beliefs, officers are instructed to transport the inmate to the prison's medical facility for further evaluation. Physical restraint and medication are utilized if needed.

Rathbun explained that corrections training at the Cranston facility now incorporate up to sixteen hours of initial crisis intervention training and four hours of annual training in role-playing and verbal de-escalation techniques. Role-plays include senior corrections officers acting out crisis scenarios. The nine-week program also incorporates up to three weeks of on-the-job training before the new officer is allowed to work alone. New recruits are videotaped during role-plays and are critiqued by instructors. Role-play scenarios are also utilized In many police trainings as well. Role-play is by far the best way to teach these skills to officers. Role-plays place officers is similar situations they will face in real life. This intensive corrections training program also teaches recruits how to differentiate symptoms of mental illness from behaviors typical of inmates who are not mentally ill.

Mentally ill inmates have more difficulty following prison rules and directives, especially when they are in crisis, according to Rathbun. Mentally ill inmates oftentimes misperceive and misevaluate the actions of others and have a distorted perception of reality. When placed in a prison setting, they may act out fears and misperceptions, leading to reoccurring rule violations. Assisting the mentally ill inmate in accessing appropriate mental health care while he or she is incarcerated is humane, and simply put, it is the right thing to do.

## Hands-On Phase Techniques (Red Light)

I will not go into great detail in this section, as my advice here is to follow your instincts, training, and your agency's protocols for the use of force. I will offer some suggestions based on my experience and the experiences of my law enforcement colleagues.

In assessing the need to go hands-on, officers again should follow their instincts. It is a good idea to follow your department's use of force protocols when dealing with a physically aggressive suspect/inmate is highly recommended. The following officer safety tips have been found helpful, and they would serve as good additions to all protocols in the use of force and physical restraint. You may see this information presented again in the chapter covering psychosis and excited delirium.

- Do not act alone! Make sure you have enough assistance on hand before you go hands-on if time permits. Having a plan (limb assignments) can both prevent injury and provide a more effective restraint. Make sure each limb in secured, and assign one officer to restrain the individual's head to prevent biting.

Human bites can cause lots of pain and discomfort as well as unwanted infections.

+ Always maintain an open airway. Turning the individual's head to the side when he or she is facedown is recommended.

+ Avoid applying direct heavy pressure to the back or the back of the neck of the person being restrained to avoid impairing his or her breathing. Applying heavy pressure, usually with a knee, can cause a condition called positional asphyxia. This is a life-threatening condition that has been known to cause sudden death. Sit up the individual as soon as you have secured him or her. These steps may avoid in-custody deaths, protecting both the suspect and the officers involved.

+ Always have backup available. Sometimes all it takes is a show of force to get an individual experiencing mental illness, or anyone for that matter, to agree to your plan.

+ Stay in good physical shape. Officers in poor shape often are injured during restraints. This includes keeping your cardiovascular system in peak condition through swimming, running, elliptical, and daily walking.

+ Take martial arts classes. While this isn't mandatory as part of your training, it will definitely help you stay fit and prepared for physical confrontations. I earned my black belt in Tang Soo Do at age fifty, proving that it is never too late to learn a new skill!

# CHAPTER 2

# WHAT IS PSYCHOSIS?

When we see individuals behave strangely or contrary to the norms of society, we often label the behavior as crazy or psychotic. This is also true when we hear about horrific or violent crimes. It is well known that the majority of crimes committed in the United States are not committed by individuals who have a psychotic disorder. Unfortunately when a person with psychosis does commit a violent crime, it is highly publicized by the media. Psychosis is a term used to describe thoughts and behaviors that are not based in reality. Individuals who are psychotic may exhibit thinking or behaviors such as believing microchips were implanted in them, hearing the voice of Satan, or believing that there is a secret plan or plot to destroy them. Psychosis is most associated with severe and persistent mental disorders, such as schizophrenia and bipolar disorder. Psychosis may also develop in individuals who are not mentally ill. Stimulant drugs, such as cocaine, PCP, bath salts, or amphetamines, have been known to cause psychosis in some individuals. Medical disorders affecting the brain, such as Parkinson's disease, Alzheimer's disease, or head injuries can also cause psychotic symptoms.

It is common for the general public and some law enforcement officers to use words such as "nuts," "loony tunes," or just plain "wacked" to describe psychosis. These terms are often used by individuals who have a poor understanding of the behaviors associated with mental illness. For some it is easier to make fun of something or someone rather than spending time learning about what they don't know. Before getting into the specifics of what happens to a person who becomes psychotic, it is first important to illustrate how the pubic misunderstanding and stigma regarding psychosis may occur, especially in relation to violent crime. In 1995 a women killed her two young children in an effort to revive a failing relationship with her boyfriend. The woman claimed that a man stole her car and kidnapped her children. It was later reported that the woman drove her car to a river's edge and proceeded to guide the vehicle into the river with her children in the backseat. The woman eventually confessed to committing the murders. She was sentenced to life in prison. Her actions were described by many as being crazy, because how could anyone in their right mind do such a thing? The woman also claimed that she had mental health issues that severely impaired her judgment at the time of the crime. Her actions that day were not driven by hallucinations or false delusional beliefs, as seen in psychotic disorders, but they were driven by her own self-interest. She methodically planned her crime, developed a fictional story about what took place to deceive police, and had a clear motive, all characteristics of nonpsychotic criminals. We also see other examples of nonpsychotic homicides committed by individuals known as serial killers. Serial killers, such as Ted Bundy (who preyed on young coeds), John Wayne Gacy (who preyed on young men), BTK (who stalked and killed women and children) and even Jeffery Dahmer (the flesh-eating killer), were all highly organized, nonpsychotic killers. Serial killers during their killing sprees are usually clear thinking (not confused or disorganized), well organized, scheming, manipulative, deceitful, and functional people who conceal their evil intent. When interviewed by investigators, the thinking of most serial killers is clear, reality-based, and free of the disorganization, hallucinations, and delusions seen in

21

psychosis. The serial killer can usually be diagnosed with a condition making the person a sexual sadist. While most individuals experience sexual pleasure from nonviolent sex, the sexual sadist can only achieve sexual satisfaction by causing pain, suffering, and death of another human being. As sick as this may sound, in most cases of serial homicides the individual is not psychotic.

There are also high numbers of workplace shootings committed by nonpsychotic, angry, and misguided individuals who feel wronged by their employers, ex-spouses, or society in general. The evil committed by these murderers along with the acts of other criminals like serial rapists and pedophiles are also most often committed by individuals who are not mentally ill. These nonpsychotic killers and the crimes they commit have something in common—motive! Motives can include greed, jealously, anger, revenge, justification (in the eyes of the killer), personal gain, satisfaction, and/or pleasure (serial killers). There also is usually no history of psychosis, mental health treatment, or psychiatric hospitalizations prior to the criminal acts. And as I stated earlier, there is no evidence of psychotic thinking during or after the crime.

The media also doesn't help in eliminating the stigma surrounding mental illness, as most media outlets perpetrate this stigma and/or confuse events involving the mentally ill.

It is important to again state that the majority of individuals experiencing psychosis do not commit homicide, sexual assault, or violent crime as stated previously. So what is psychosis, and how can an officer recognize this condition?

Every day in this country law enforcement officers come in contact with individuals suffering from mental illness while they are performing their duties in communities or correctional facilities. While many officers view these encounters as nuisances or wastes of time, veteran officers have learned through experience that, if not handled well, these situations can quickly escalate into a deadly force encounter, especially when the individual is experiencing a psychotic episode.

As mentioned earlier, psychosis is a term used to describe a person whose thoughts are not based in reality. Individuals who present psychotic may experience auditory hallucinations, such as hearing voices or maintain bizarre false beliefs called delusions. While the most common cause of psychosis is a mental illness called schizophrenia, drugs and certain medical conditions have also been known to cause psychosis. Stimulant drugs like cocaine and amphetamines as well as hallucinogens like PCP have been known to cause both delusions and hallucinations. These illicit drugs are known to overexcite brain regions that are responsible for judgment as well as controlling behaviors and impulse control. Drugs also interfere with the brain's ability to process sights, sounds, and sensations coming into the brain that help us determine fact from fiction.

Chemicals called neurotransmitters are also negatively affected by drugs of abuse. Neurotransmitters, which help nerve cells communicate, are released by the brain to either turn on (or speed up) certain brain or body processes such as thinking, running, or keeping our mood stable. Neurotransmitters also slow down processes such as to promote relaxation and peace of mind. In psychosis, it is believed that these chemicals may be released in larger amounts throughout the brain, causing nerve cells to misfire and become overwelmed. When nerve cells are overstimulated, they can cause the brain to misread and misevaluate the information it is taking in, which can lead to psychotic symptoms such as delusions and hallucinations. Stimulant drugs are also known to cause a person's fight-or-flight response to go on overdrive, giving individuals increased fear, strength, and stamina. It is common for this drug-induced psychosis to also cause paranoid thoughts, such as believing one's food is poisoned or believing that one is being followed or persecuted by others.

Drug-induced psychosis usually remits in twenty-four to seventy-two hours, which is the time is takes for the drug to clear a person's system. So a psychotic individual picked up by police, running naked across a busy street (who is under the influence of drugs), will usually return back to normal (a nonpsychotic state) in a day or two. It is also a dead giveaway that drugs are the cause of psychosis when a person's urine test is positive for drugs at the time of the incident.

Certain medical conditions that cause brain tissue destruction, such as Alzheimer's disease, Parkinson's disease, Huntington's chorea, head injuries, and brain tumors, are all known to cause psychosis. It is believed that neurotransmitter levels (as mentioned in the section about drug abuse) as well as brain circuitry can be negatively affected by these medical conditions, causing the individual to hallucinate or experience delusional thoughts. Some prescribed medications as well as herbal remedies have also been known to cause time-limited symptoms of psychosis. Psychotic thinking could also present in individuals suffering from recent head injuries or untreated medical conditions. This is why it is important for all individuals with psychotic thinking to have physical exams and blood work as part of diagnostic workups, as psychosis due to either of the above causes can usually be reversed.

Schizophrenia is the most common psychotic disorder which occurs in 1% of the U.S. adult population according to the National Institute of Mental Health. While science is not sure of what causes schizophrenia, experts tell us a combination of genetic factors (runs in families), medical complications of pregnancy (virus, flu, lack of oxygen), and possibly environmental factors (severe abuse, stressors) may cause the disease to manifest. Schizophrenia is a chronic and disabling brain disease which is believed to physically attack the brain, causing abnormal brain development and functioning. Schizophrenia usually begins in late adolescence or early twenties. It is believed that environmental stressors experienced during this stage of life—dating, enduring relationship breakups, leaving home for college, and joining the military—may cause the illness to develop in certain individuals with genetic predispositions to schizophrenia. As the illness progresses, brain circuits responsible for communication, judgment, impulse control, and emotional expression are affected. This is one reason why individuals with this disorder may impulsively strike out, may be unable to clearly express their thoughts, may present with inappropriate emotions, or may present overly fearful or confused.

Individuals with schizophrenia also begin to have difficulty differentiating reality from fiction, which may cause an individual to misperceive or misevaluate what they see, hear, and experience in their environment. Misperceiving of external experiences is believed to be the cause of delusional (false) beliefs, such as believing that one's food is poisoned or that an external force like God, the devil, or a popular political figure is controlling one's actions. Delusional beliefs may also be due to a malfunctioning of the brain's filtering system. It is believed that the thalamus, which works as an information filter or processor for the brain, and the frontal lobes, which are responsible for interpreting information and directing action may be mis-firing in schizophrenia. All incoming messages to the brain from the external world (except smell) are first received for processing through our senses (sight, sound, touch, and taste) before they are relayed to the thalamus and other brain regions for processing. The sense of smell can oftentimes bypass the thalamus, which is one reason smells, both good and bad, have a strong emotional impact. (They quickly access emotional memory.) If the brain's filtering system is working properly, the frontal lobe region of the brain can both accurately read the information it receives and relay this information to the appropriate part of the brain, directing logical and rational actions.

In schizophrenia this filtering system malfunctions or short-circuits. This malfunction causes people to misevaluate what they see, hear, and experience in their environment. What most of us see as simple occurrences of everyday life may be misread or misevaluated by the people with schizophrenia as having specific or special meaning to them. To illustrate what happens when this filtering system malfunctions, let's take the example of two men watching a band play in a local park. One individual has schizophrenia (and is off medication) and the other does not. Both individuals are listening to the same music arrangement at an outdoor concert. The person without schizophrenia is enjoying the concert and perceives the music as both relaxing and nonthreatening. The person with schizophrenia, due to this brain filtering malfunction, hears the same music as the person who is not mentally ill but believes that the music lyrics are giving him dark messages from Satan. This person also misinterprets a smile by a band member as something that is "mocking him." He proceeds to scream out loud, "Leave me alone," and runs out of the park. The person with schizophrenia misevaluated the music as being a threat to his life, which inappropriately activated his fight-or-flight response. As mentioned earlier when a person's fight-or-flight center is activated, stress hormones are released, giving a person strength and quickness to either fight or flee the enemy. The individual with schizophrenia is convinced that the only lifesaving option is to leave the park to prevent impending doom.

So as you can see from the previous example, the illness of schizophrenia may cause an individual to misevaluate, misinterpret, and possibly overreact to situations in his or her environment, causing irrational behaviors and actions. Delusions or false beliefs are also common because of this malfunction. The most common delusion is paranoia. Paranoid individuals may believe that they are being followed, persecuted, and spied upon or that the world may be coming to an end.

The home environment of a person with psychosis may also give clues to the severity of paranoia. Responding officers may see doors and windows nailed shut, or blankets placed over TV sets. Often times baseball bats, knives, bats or pipes are in hallways or near bedrooms. Tin foil may also be placed throughout the house due to the person believing that dangerous radio waves are entering the house. As I mentioned earlier, individuals with Schizophrenia have a low incidence of committing violent crime. What we do see in practice is a slightly higher risk of violence occurring when individuals with Schizophrenia have a past history of violence, are actively using drugs or alcohol or are not receiving or refuse to take medication. So while the violence rate for schizophrenia is lower than that seen in the general population, there have been cases of individuals with schizophrenia committing violent crimes. In April of 2007 Seung-Hui Cho, the perpetrator of the Virginia Tech massacre killed thirty-two people in a murderous rampage. His behaviors prior to the shooting suggest psychosis. His writings, which were discovered after the shooting, and his self-made video, which he sent to the media, were filled with paranoid ideas. Statements about how the "world was against him" were common themes. He would take random pictures of students, ride his bike in circles at night, stalk female students, sit for long hours and stare out of his dorm window, and write about dark and paranoid themes in his class essays. Based on the information made available in media reports, Seung-Hui Cho appeared to have a psychotic disorder. Cho also appeared to have had a long history of psychiatric difficulties beginning in childhood. Cho's disturbing pattern of escalating and frightening behaviors had many of the people he had contact with very concerned. Finally in 2005 after many reports of bizarre behavior on campus, he was deemed mentally ill by a judge and court-ordered to seek treatment. It does not appear that he followed this order, and reports are sketchy as to the actions or inactions of mental health and law enforcement authorities. Many questions remain in this case. Firstly psychotic individuals with threatening and paranoid behaviors like Seung-Hui Cho should be taken into protective custody and taken to the nearest emergency room for psychiatric assessment. It is also important for officers to clearly document and report to emergency room staff all behaviors reported or observed, including behaviors of violence, threats, or self-abuse. These behaviors place a person at risk to self or others, which gives officers the legal obligation to remove the person from the community. Court orders also need to be followed. A mental health court order mandates that the person engage in mental health counseling, but does not necessary mandate a person to take medication. A court order is useless unless it has a petition for instruction attached. A petition for instructions is an attachment to the court order that spells out which medication the person needs to take. If a person does not comply with the order, the individual is expected to be returned to the hospital until he or she voluntarily takes medication as prescribed. The goal is for psychotic individuals to consistently take daily medication called antipsychotics and receive weekly counseling. Many times it takes a court order to get this done. Law enforcement and mental health professionals need to have a coordinated game plan when individuals like Cho refuse to comply with court orders. Oftentimes law enforcement officers are unaware of individuals in their community under court-ordered treatment. Confidentiality laws restrict some information being shared with others, unless such information places an individual or community at risk of harming self or others. In this writer's opinion, based on information made available, Cho appeared to need an emergency intervention by both police and mental health. This intervention would have placed him back in front of a judge who would have most likely ordered psychiatric hospitalization. Media reports oftentimes portray perpetrators of violent crime as individuals who impulsively snap into murderous rages. In many cases similar to Cho's there is a long pattern of dysfunctional behavior or thinking prior to the crime. As also seen in the Virginia Tech shooting, people just don't snap!

In January 2013 a sixty-five-year-old man with a long history of violent and aggressive behavior boarded a school bus and demanded the bus driver give him two young boys ages six and eight. The bus driver heroically refused but was eventually shot and killed by the assailant. The man kidnapped a five-year-old boy and fled to a bunker located on his property. Police and FBI negotiators attempted to talk the man into letting the boy go without success. Fortunately the boy was rescued as police eventually entered the bunker, and after an apparent struggle the suspect was shot and killed. Could this incident have been prevented? Was the man exhibiting non-psychotic criminal behavior, or was he psychotic? These and other questions were asked at this time of this incident with the hope of uncovering the motive for this crime. As I stated earlier, high-functioning, nonaggressive individuals do not impulsively get up one morning and decide to commit homicide or other heinous crimes. These individuals usually have a history of violence or unusual behaviors prior to these incidents happening. In this case the individual lived alone and apparently had a long history of making threats to children and adult neighbors. Here is a listing of problematic behaviors noted prior to this incident:

+ The man killed a neighbor's dog with a lead pipe for being on his property.
+ He patrolled his property at night with a flashlight and shot off his gun.
+ Neighbors described him as being paranoid of others.
+ He discharged his firearm at neighbors who drove past his house.
+ He was awaiting a court date for this incident.

- Neighbors reported seeing him in town staring as if he was looking right through them.
- He would often threaten to shoot children who went near or on his property.
- He had an elaborate underground bunker on his property.
- Neighbors reported seeing him carrying large cinder blocks and digging in his yard on a daily basis.

As you can see by the behaviors previously listed, this man clearly had had some form of a psychiatric disturbance that was characterized by paranoid thoughts. His paranoid beliefs and aggression toward others appears to have reached psychotic proportions. This level of paranoia, if allowed to go untreated, places a person at serious risk of harming either self or others. If this man's beliefs were psychotic in nature, they may have included irrational fears, such as believing his neighbors were plotting against him, spreading rumors about him, or planning to kill him. Individuals with this type of paranoia may eventually become so fearful and desperate that they lash out at others to protect themselves against perceived harm. Remember, in psychotic disorders individuals truly believe that their delusional thoughts are real! As stated, this man had a pending court date for shooting at adults and children in his neighborhood. While we don't know if his arrest and pending court appearance precipitated the homicide and kidnapping, individuals have acted in desperation in the past when faced with jail time. His aggression, paranoia, repeated threats to others, and possession of a firearm placed him at high risk to commit a violent act. He appeared to meet criteria for involuntary hospitalization as was the case with Cho. While this man's mental condition is still unknown, he does appear to suffer from some form of mental illness. This incident ended with law enforcement officers needing to charge the bunker because of further concern that the man's temperament or behaviors were worsening. It is not fully clear if the man either shot himself or was killed by police. The good news is that the five-year-old child was recovered physically unharmed.

It's also common for paranoid individuals to believe that their household appliances, telephones, TVs, or computers have been tampered with by an outside force. They may also believe that they are being monitored by the government. You may see paranoid individuals nail or board up windows and doors in an attempt to keep their pursuers at bay. Grandiose delusions may also be present. Grandiosity is the belief that a person has special powers, gifts, or talents that are unique. James Holmes, the Aurora, Colorado, movie theater killer who, during the opening of a new Batman movie, entered the theater heavily armed, killing twelve and injuring fifty-eight patrons appeared to have grandiose thoughts. He allegedly believed he was the Joker on a special mission on the night of the shootings, which appears to be a grandiose delusion. While not much information regarding Holmes's current mental state is being disclosed, Holmes, like Cho, may have had an undiagnosed and untreated psychotic disorder. When one believes that he or she has special powers, gifts, and talents or when the person believes he or she is a famous person or celebrity, these are examples of grandiose delusions. Individuals with grandiosity may also believe that they can solve world hunger or that they have discovered the cure for cancer. They often feel they can influence the weather or have the ability to fly.

Individuals may also have delusions of reference where they believe that something in the environment has personal and special meaning to them. For example, they may believe that a message on a billboard that others may see as having no personal meaning (other than trying to persuade us to buy a product) was intended specifically for them. Or they may hear a song on the radio and believe that the singer is speaking directly to them. Delusions of control occur when people believe that they are receiving messages from an outside force like a local radio tower. They may believe that the radio tower is instructing them to dig ditches in their backyards. This type of delusion can make people highly unpredictable and possibly dangerous to themselves or others, as they believe they have no control over their thoughts and actions.

It's important to understand that to psychotic individuals their delusional beliefs are real, as their malfunctioning brains tell them so. It is also common for individuals to seek validation of their beliefs by contacting law enforcement or writing letters to politicians. Eventually when they feel they are not being taken seriously by authorities, they may take matters into their own hands. Such was the case of Russell Weston Jr. In 1999 Russell Weston shot and killed two US Capitol police officers and carried a diagnosis of schizophrenia. Weston's delusional thoughts involved the belief that President Clinton was operating a time machine in the White House and was planning to detonate a bomb over Montana. After government officials stopped responding to his letters, he stole his father's handgun and traveled to the capitol, where he shot and killed two capitol police officers. Investigators discovered Weston had a long history of psychosis that included paranoid delusions and violent actions as already stated. He also had a history of psychiatric hospitalizations and mental health involvement, which made it unlikely that he fabricated the psychosis to avoid prosecution. The more recent shootings at Virginia Tech and the Aurora movie theater appear similar to the Weston case. Both Individuals appeared obsessed with their delusional beliefs as was Weston. Their beliefs also began to affect their ability to appropriately communicate with others, which lead to both individuals being banned from their respected college campuses for bizarre and possible psychotic presentations.

Hallucinations are also common in psychosis. We believe that the malfunctioning brain begins to create strange sounds and voices that the person experiences as real. These sounds and voices are not real, but the person experiences them as real. Individuals experiencing auditory hallucinations (hearing voices and sounds) appear distracted and may quickly look in the direction they believe the sound/voice is coming from. When individuals are hallucinating, their speech may abruptly stop in midsentence as they attempt to listen to the strange sounds. Individuals with schizophrenia who hallucinate may also shout back at the voices or place cotton balls in both ears to block them out. Cotton balls are not effective, as the hallucination is being generated inside the person's head as opposed to coming from the outside. Sometimes hallucinations are of a command nature. They may instruct the person to carry out certain actions, such as throwing a brick through a window or in the some extreme cases directing the person to jump out a window or to stab themselves. In the 1970s Herbert Mullin, diagnosed with schizophrenia, experienced command hallucinations telling him to kill. Mullin believed that by killing others, he could prevent future earthquakes and thusly save the world. He also felt that he was receiving telepathic secret messages linking him to Albert Einstein and future catastrophic events. His voices commanded him to kill a local pastor along with twelve others until he was finally brought to justice. Psychotic individuals can also experience visual hallucinations (seeing strange shapes), taste hallucinations (tasting gasoline), or touch hallucination (bugs crawling on the skin). Remember, the person is actually experiencing these frightening and confusing sensations.

In September 2013, a thirty-four-year US Navy veteran entered a Washington, DC, naval shipyard with a shotgun and randomly opened fire, killing twelve people and wounding eight. The man was killed during a shootout with police. It is unclear at the time of this writing if he killed himself or was shot by police. According to media reports, this man had a history of mental health issues and allegedly received treatment at the VA since August 2013. On August 7, 2013, the man called police from a hotel room in Newport, RI, requesting assistance, as he believed three men were shooting waves into his body to prevent him from sleeping. He also complained of hearing voices at the time of the call, according to police reports. It also is alleged that the man did receive a psychiatric evaluation in 2013 during which he disclosed that he was hearing voices that were telling him to kill people. His history also revealed the following behaviors:

- In 2004 he was arrested for shooting out the tires on the car of a fellow contractor.
- In 2010 he was arrested for firing shots inside his apartment.
- He was released early from the navy for misconduct that included insubordination, disorderly conduct, and absent without leave.
- He had an apparent history of paranoia and sleep difficulties.
- His father believed he had a history of PTSD from being at the World Trade Center during 9/11.

It is likely that this man experienced a psychotic break characterized by auditory hallucinations (command hallucinations telling him to kill) and paranoid delusions (three men shooting waves at him). But why did this man not get hospitalized by the mental health professionals if the reports of him disclosing he was having auditory hallucinations to kill people were accurate? Also why did police on August 7 not take him to an ER to be evaluated based on his presentation that night? If reports are accurate, this man appeared to meet criteria to be hospitalized against his will (involuntary certification). Police may have had enough information to take him into protective custody and transport him to an ER for evaluation. Please don't mis-understand me – I was not there! I am not Monday morning quarterbacking this case to lay blame on police or mental health authorities, rather I am presenting what we know about this case to help raise awareness in future cases with similar profiles.

In 2012 twenty-year-old Adam Lanza walked into Sandy Hook Elementary School and fatally shot and killed twenty children and six school employees. After the killings he committed suicide while he was still in the school. Prior to the shootings, Lanza was described as an anxious and socially awkward loner who exhibited behavioral disturbances prior to the incident. He apparently was obsessed with violent video games and military weaponry and had access to firearms— an accident waiting to happen! It is not known whether Adam Lanza was psychotic, depressed, or suffering from another form of mental illness. The fact that his mother was thinking of involuntarily hospitalizing him, his shooting of young children, and eventual suicide are indicators that he had some type of emotionally disturbance.

In December 2013, the Connecticut state police released documents to the public regarding the Newtown shooting that provided more information about the shooter, Adam Lanza. The following information regarding Lanza's psychiatric and behavioral history was obtained from these documents. Lanza's father described him as a "happy kid" who did well in school. The father also reported that his son began to change around age eleven, appearing sad and anxious. Lanza also began having difficulty dealing with stress and frustration and would oftentimes isolate himself from others. Despite appearing depressed, his father reported that Lanza was never aggressive. His work in school also began to decline around this time, and teachers reported his writings to be "disturbing" as well as "violent and graphic." He also was obsessed with war, guns, and battles. He also wrote short stories (*The Big Book of Granny*) that depicted a sociopathic grandmother who performed hateful and extremely violent acts toward kids and adults. According to the reports, Lanza was exposed to firearms at a young age, and in one photo released, Lanza, who appeared around four years old, is seen dressed in hunting attire, draped with ammunition, and holding a handgun.

His first psychiatric evaluation occurred in 2006. At that time the evaluating psychiatrist referred him to a nurse practitioner for medication. He apparently was seen for four visits and prescribed Celexa, an antidepressant. Reports state that his mother, Mary Lanza, discontinued his medication, as she felt he was experiencing side effects. He was diagnosed with profound autism and was noted to be "emotionally paralyzed" by obsessive compulsive disorder. Obsessive compulsive disorder, also known as OCD, is a severe anxiety disorder that causes a person to have distressing and repeated thoughts. While this is not considered a psychotic disorder, OCD behavior's can reach psychosis in certain cases. Individuals with OCD usually attempt to rid themselves of these distressing thoughts by engaging in daily rituals such as repeated hand washing, checking locks, or excessive cleaning. Lanza's OCD symptoms included changing his socks up to twenty times a day, requiring his mother to do three loads of laundry a day. He also wouldn't touch doorknobs. He would wash his hands often and would shower multiple times each day. It also was reported that he didn't experience physical pain when he was injured and that he was sensitive to light.

Academically he was very bright. Reports state that he eventually needed to leave school at age sixteen because he had multiple disputes with teachers and fellow students. While Nancy Lanza denied he was aggressive, she warned her babysitter to "never turn your back on him." At home he only communicated with his mother via e-mail and very rarely came out of his room. Prior to the shooting, he was in his room 24-7 (for three months straight), and his mother voiced concerns to friends that he was becoming increasingly more despondent. Allegedly his mother took him to the shooting range in an attempt to bond with him because of his interest/obsession with firearms. He also felt that his mother cared more for the children at Sandy Hook, where she had a history of volunteering, than she did for him, which might have fed his motive. According to reports, Nancy Lanza had multiple semiautomatic weapons and ammunition in the house (1,700 rounds of ammunition). Prior to the shooting at Sandy Hook Adam Lanza shot and killed his mother before leaving for the school. The incident ended with him committing suicide, shooting himself at the scene.

It does appear from the above history that Adam Lanza had several issues occurring at once. He appeared to have a form of autism that at the time of his evaluation was known as Asperger's. Asperger's is now grouped in a category of developmental disorders called autism spectrum disorders and is seen as a higher-functioning form of autism. Autism is covered in more detail in chapter 15. So while Lanza was diagnosed with autism, he also appeared to be suffering from depression and a severe anxiety disorder known as OCD as stated above. It is common for individuals suffering from depression to be preoccupied with death, sadness, hopelessness, and at times violence or suicide. The fact that he killed himself at the scene is a clue that he may have been suffering from severe depression.

Getting back to Schizophrenia, It is important to keep in mind that the majority of individuals diagnosed with schizophrenia *do not commit heinous crimes* as those seen in the previous cases. In fact, only 3 to 5 percent of violence in the general population is attributed to those with severe and persistent mental illness such as schizophrenia (*New England Journal of Medicine*, November, 16 2006, Dr. Richard Freeman). Unfortunately the cases involving schizophrenics usually get lots of media attention, giving the general public the false impression that all schizophrenics are violent. In fact, the majority of violent crimes in the United States today, especially against women, are committed by adults who are not mentally ill. We also know that mass murder deaths are far less than single homicides. The Congressional Research Service/ FBI also reports that there have been seventy-eight mass public shootings in the past thirty years, which resulted in 547 deaths and 559,347 (single homicides) murders during the same time span. So less than 1 percent of total murders in the past thirty years occurred because of mass public shootings!

We also know that we cannot predict violence based solely on a diagnosis. Violence is predicted based on past history of violence. Simply put, if people have assaulted others in the past, they are more likely to do it again in the future. So while being psychotic doesn't necessarily mean people will commit violence, what we do know is that when people with psychosis go off their medication (with a history of violence) or are not on medication as in many of the cases above, the chance of violence occurring goes up. So accessing treatment for someone with psychosis needs to be viewed as an urgent medical problem requiring immediate care and treatment.

Statistics also show that suicide is far more common in individuals with schizophrenia than homicide and that schizophrenics have high rates of being exploited, assaulted, and murdered by others, especially those who are homeless. Studies consistently show that individuals with schizophrenia are no more dangerous than the general population as long as they are taking prescribed medication and being seen by a mental health professional one to two times per week. The problem with this plan is that many individuals with schizophrenia either refuse to take medication or are not taking their medication as prescribed. Many do not take their medication because they do not feel that they are sick. As mentioned earlier, the frontal cortex of the brain is responsible for judgment, planning, and insight. Insight is the ability to understand and find solutions to problems. Since the person's frontal cortex is impaired in schizophrenia, this ability is lacking. Without these abilities psychotic individuals oftentimes have poor hygiene and poor nutrition, and they wear dirty clothes. They can dress inappropriately for the season, employ poor money management skills, and refuse medical and/or psychiatric treatment for serious conditions. This also is the reason many individuals with schizophrenia end up alone and homeless.

Medications do not cure schizophrenia. Medicines called antipsychotics are prescribed for all causes of psychosis (drug, medical, and psychiatric). Antipsychotics, also known as major tranquilizers, work by restabilizing the chemical imbalances found in schizophrenia. They reduce the hallucinations, delusions, and behavioral disturbances associated with psychosis. Antipsychotics are available in pill form, quick-dissolving tablets, and in long-acting injectable medication. Many times individuals with psychosis will try to deceive health-care workers into believing they are taking their medication. Individuals accomplish this by a technique called *cheeking*. Cheeking is a term used to describe the situation when a person purposely does not swallow a pill. People attempt to fool the mental health workers by putting the pills between their cheeks and gums, appearing to swallow. When the workers leave, these individuals spit out the pills. In order to address cheeking, a quick-dissolving tablet was created. The tablet instantly dissolves on the tongue, eliminating the cheeking concern. If individuals refuse all oral medication, which is common, injectable antipsychotics are available. Individuals are given an intramuscular injection in either their arm or buttocks. The big advantage of using injectable medication is that the medicine will stay in the person's system for several weeks, depending on the brand of medication. This injectable technology, introduced in the 1980s, was groundbreaking in the field, as it ensured the medication remained in people's systems whether they agreed to take their pills or not. If individuals refuse all medications, including injectable medication, hospitalization or court-ordered treatment should be explored. Being aware of these new advances are important for law enforcement officers who oftentimes are called to intervene with psychotic individuals after they have not taken their antipsychotic oral pills. While officers can't prescribe medication, they certainly can ask the mental health professional to consider a long-acting injection as opposed to pills. Many times this one intervention will significantly reduce both community incidents and police interventions, making it safer for both the psychotic individual and the responding officers.

There are several kinds of medication for psychosis. I will list here the most common prescribed. Older medications are as follows:

- Haldol
- Prolixin
- Trilafon
- Navane

Newer medications are most often prescribed and are as follows:

- Clozaril
- Risperdal
- Zyprexa
- Seroquel
- Abilify
- Saphris
- Invega

The following medications are available in long acting injectables:

- Prolixin Decanoate
- Haldol Decanoate

- ◆ Risperdal Consta
- ◆ Invega Sustenna
- ◆ Zyprexa Relprevv

It is important to keep in mind that mental health professionals may not think of giving individuals injectable medication, believing their patients are taking medications as prescribed. There also are inexperienced workers entering the field each day who are not adequately trained in recognizing medication noncompliance. Injectable medications should be considered for all individuals with psychosis who experience multiple relapses and psychiatric hospitalizations because they are not taking their medications. From the information made available in the previously mentioned cases, it does not appear that any of the killers were on antipsychotic medication at the time they committed their crimes.

How is it that none of the above killers were in treatment? Were there warning signs? It is common for individuals with psychosis to isolate or shun contact with others because of their delusional beliefs, so it is quite possible that they flew under the radar of authorities to some extent. As we've seen in all these cases, the behavior of the untreated psychotic individual usually worsens without treatment. It is well known that when individuals with psychosis begin to approach or confront others regarding their delusional beliefs, it is time to seek an emergency evaluation. As stated earlier, under mental health laws in most states, people can be hospitalized against their will if they are suffering from mental disorders like schizophrenia and seem to be a danger to others or place their health and safety in jeopardy because of their psychosis. This gives the mental health professional some leeway if the person denies suicide or homicide ideation. The "health in jeopardy" wording was added to the involuntary certification document in some states approximately twenty years ago to allow mental health professionals to hospitalize individuals against their will who were psychotic but not necessarily threatening to kill themselves or others. For example, psychotic individuals who were walking in the middle of the street, not eating, tampering with electrical wiring or gas appliances, or setting fires in their apartment could be hospitalized against their will. Hospitalizing people against their will is known as involuntary certification. Some states have widened this criterion to include individuals in need of treatment as determined by a mental health professional. It's a good idea to check with your local state mental health authority to review how the mental health law applies in your state.

In most states qualified mental health professionals and physicians have the authority to hospitalize people against their will. This process can hold an individual in a hospital for up to ten days. Individuals will receive a psychiatric evaluation and medication when hospitalized. It is important to note that individuals are not medicated against their will unless they are highly agitated, threatening, or violent when they are in the hospital. If the hospital feels that the individual needs to be forced into treatment, which should include medication, the staff can apply for a civil court commitment. In most states, a civil court commitment is a process that involves the hospital psychiatrist presenting a case to the court to obtain court-ordered treatment. The court order should hold the person for a longer stay and should include what is called a petition for instructions. Petition for instruction, as stated earlier, will list the medication the person is being court-ordered to take. Remember, if these individuals are not violent, suicidal, or aggressive while in the hospital, they may not receive medication and will often be released to the community after brief hospital stays. This can be a highly frustrating process that often is repeated until the person accepts treatment.

So while it is not easy to force a psychotic individual into treatment, it is within the law for a law enforcement officer to take a psychotic individual into custody for evaluation. This will most likely occur at the local emergency room. In correction facilities, mental health clinicians are usually available to conduct these evaluations. Again it is important to alert the mental health clinician of all behaviors witnessed. This information will be needed to build a case for involuntary hospitalization if the person is not suicidal or homicidal. As I said earlier, behaviors demonstrating risks to health and safety need to be communicated to medical and mental health professionals to support the need for involuntary commitment.

So leaving an individual with psychosis untreated, as we saw in the previously mentioned cases, can have disastrous results for the psychotic individual and the community at large.

As a law enforcement officer, it is important to understand when a person with psychosis may be in need of hospitalization. The following is a listing of warning signs that may indicate impending violence or behaviors that could place the individual at risk to him or herself and others.

+ The person may have a previous history of violence toward others. This is the most important warning sign, as history often repeats itself. Information on past history can be acquired by family members, previous police or corrections involvement, and mental health professionals.
+ The person presents highly agitated, suspicious, and fearful when he or she is expressing delusional thoughts. The individual may also yell, throw objects, or disrobe.
+ The person may have paranoid delusions of being followed, being spied upon, or being the victim of someone poisoning his or her food. These individuals may also believe that their neighbors are

laughing at them, that neighborhood children are mocking them, or that local pastors are sending them telepathic threats.

- The person may have delusions of being controlled by an external force such as receiving commanding messages from a local radio tower.

- The individual may be receiving command hallucinations instructing him or her to engage in dangerous acts such as jumping out a window, stabbing a neighbor, etc. It is important to know if hallucinations are of a commanding nature.

- The person may be obsessed, delusional, or preoccupied with bladed weapons or firearms.

- The person may express a wish to die or hurt others.

- These individuals may believe they have romantic relationships with people either whom they have not met or whom they had brief insignificant encounters with (insignificant to the victim, not the perpetrator). This type of delusion often involves celebrities, athletes, or politicians. This oftentimes is called "psychotic stalking," as the perpetrator's thoughts are not based in reality.

- Individuals with psychosis may have made frequent attempts to contact law enforcement or government officials in an attempt to validate their delusional beliefs (e.g., letter writing, phone calls, etc.).

- The psychotic individual is naked or disrobing in public.

Remember, having psychotic individuals transported by rescue to a local emergency room is most often the correct course of action when evidence of these behaviors exists. Officers should clearly document the psychotic behaviors evident at the scene and report all such behaviors to emergency room staff. It is also important to make a case for involuntary certification, which can be supported by behaviors that place the person and the community at risk. Yes, officers can make this recommendation, which will make it a bit more difficult to release the person back to the community after evaluation. Statements such as, "This man is clearly a danger to himself and others and meets criteria to be hospitalized against his will based on behaviors we witnessed at the scene." Remember; it is important to state the behaviors and to announce that you will be documenting your concerns because of the severity of the situation. This approach can sway the decision from releasing to hospitalizing the individual.

# CHAPTER 3

# EXCITED DELIRIUM

I briefly mentioned earlier the term *excited delirium*. Individuals in an excited delirium state are often experiencing psychotic symptoms. While the medical profession is slow to recognize this condition, law enforcement officers have faced numerous individuals with this syndrome. Most often individuals in an excited delirium state present as bizarre, naked, and strong as a bull!

While medical professionals are not 100 percent sure of the cause of excited delirium, several common disorders have been known to cause this condition. The use of stimulant drugs such as cocaine, methamphetamines, PCP, bath salts, and synthetic marijuana are well known to cause excited delirium. Let's take a closer look on how drugs cause this condition. Upon entering the body, stimulant drugs like cocaine rapidly excite brain regions responsible for movement, behavior, anxiety, fear, and aggression. Stimulants also increase adrenalin levels, producing increased energy, strength, and endurance, which are also common features of excited delirium. In some individuals—and we're still not sure why—drug administration may cause an unexpected massive release of brain-stimulating neurotransmitters (not normally expected by the drug), and/or a person's body may rapidly overheat because of excessive stimulation. Narcotics rarely cause an excited delirium state.

Narcotics such as heroin, opiates, and morphine work by producing relaxation and sedation, which is the opposite effect of stimulants such as cocaine.

*Bath salts* are drugs that are also known to cause excited delirium. These substances are oftentimes confused with the bath salts used in bathing, namely Epsom salt. The manufactures of these elicit and dangerous drugs call them bath salts to make it easier to sell the drugs legally to smoke shops and convenience store owners. Bath salts contain potent stimulant like substances called cathinones. Mephedrone along with a substance known as MDPV are cathinones found in bath salts. Like cocaine, bath salts overexcite brain circuits. Bath salts also have been associated with extremely bizarre, psychotic, and violent behavior. The recent case of a man, who viciously attacked and began eating the face of a homeless man, was believed to be under the influence of bath salts at the time of the attack. This was a case of excited delirium. Bath salts are very dangerous drugs that are now banned in many states.

Another drug known to cause an excited delirium is synthetic marijuana, also known as K2 or spice. This drug is marketed as a safe or natural high and is found in many smoke shops here in the United States. Made to look like potpourri and falsely sold as herbal/natural marijuana, this drug is not marijuana at all. The active drug, identified as JWH-018 or JWH-073, can be up to four to a hundred times more potent than marijuana. This drug has also been known to cause excited delirium states manifested by extreme paranoia, aggression, and psychosis. This is an extremely dangerous drug that unfortunately causes users, many in their late teens to early twenties, to require emergency room care. The good news is that the DEA recently placed many of the ingredients found in bath salts and synthetic marijuana on the list of substances illegal to purchase here in the US. Unfortunately, illegal drug manufactures often modify the chemical formulations of these products attempting to deceive federal drug enforcement officials and consumers. For example, new bath salt formulations with street names such as "Cosmic Blast" or "IPOD" are being sold as jewelry or phone screen cleaner. So with designer drug formulations changing daily it is difficult to stop the sale and manufacture of these dangerous drugs.

*PCP*, known as angel dust, is a powerful hallucinogen that can also cause an excited delirium and or psychotic state. PCP made it into the headlines recently as it was speculated that a former NFL star who allegedly had a history of PCP, according to media reports, was described as being in a possible paranoid state prior to his alleged involvement in a homicide in 2013. PCP is a powerful drug that can cause hallucinations, paranoid delusions, aggression, and excessive strength seen in many cases of excited delirium. *Ecstasy*, also known as MDMA, can also cause an excited delirium state. A powered form of ecstasy called molly was responsible for a string of deaths and several cases of excited delirium in August of 2013. The drug, which is part stimulant and part hallucinogen, can produce dangerous side effects, such as cardiac arrest and hyperthermia, as seen in other stimulant drugs.

Untreated medical conditions such as head injuries, brain tumors, toxic effects of medications, urinary tract infections (especially in the elderly), high fever, and electrolyte imbalances (sodium, potassium, etc.) have also been known to cause an acute disoriented and/or excited delirium state.

Individuals with severe and persistent mental illness, such as schizophrenia and bipolar disorder, may also present in an excited delirium. Schizophrenia and bipolar disorder are biologically based illnesses that can have cocainelike effects on the brain (without the use of drugs). It is common for these individuals to stop taking their medications, which oftentimes precipitates an excited delirium or community incident requiring police intervention.

It also appears that during an excited delirium episode, the body's internal temperature control malfunctions, causing what is termed "hyperthermia." Hyperthermia causes a person's core body temperature to rise to dangerous levels, causing profuse sweating and dehydration. This is one reason people disrobe or stay naked when approached by officers. Hyperthermia is a life-threatening condition that needs immediate medical attention!

I am often asked, "What does this disorder look like?" I guarantee most law enforcement officers have either seen or experienced close up an individual in an excited delirium state. The following is a listing of the common signs and symptoms of an individual presenting with an excited delirium?

+ *Naked or disrobing.* Remember, if people remove a hat, rings, or a watch, they are most likely getting ready to fight (criminal intent) and not in an excited delirium state! Aggressively taking off all cloths or being found naked is more common in excited delirium.
+ *Excessive sweating.* This is due to excessive body temperature.
+ *Yelling and screaming.* While an angry inmate or civilian will typically yell and scream, a combination of yelling with other symptoms such as disrobing or bizarre behavior may be more problematic. The person may also be intensely staring without blinking or may have the infamous "wild eyes."
+ *Expressed paranoia of others.* Listen for delusional content in speech, such as "They're after me" or "We're all in danger." Use the interventions listed here to reduce the person's fears, saying, "I will not let anyone hurt you," or, "I will keep you safe." Remember to keep your distance and remain vigilant!
+ *Excessive energy* or agitation/aggression.
+ *Disorganized* or rambling speech.

+ Evidence of *hallucinations*, such as complaining of bugs on the skin or shouting in the air as if speaking to someone.

+ *Delusional beliefs.* Look for odd or bizarre thoughts or ideas, such as, "I am God on a mission to save the world"!

+ *Bizarre behavior* such as pulling up shrubs in the park, destroying signs, and breaking glass. For some reason, individuals with excited delirium are often *breaking glass* when officers arrive.

+ More agitated and aggressive when *OC spray* deployed. While most folks will comply after being sprayed the excited delirium suspect most often becomes worse.

+ *Excessive strength!* This is one of the main reasons to wait for backup, as we believe that this condition excessively increases adrenalin levels, which translates into increased aggression and power.

+ *Impervious to pain!* This is why other less lethal options such as the baton or self-defense techniques are ineffective.

+ *Sudden tranquility.* Excited delirium can cause cardiac and respiratory arrest because of the combination of high temperature, high blood pressure, drugs, increased cardiac input, and physical combativeness. This is one of the main reasons to have rescue or medical personnel staged in the area.

The following officer safety tips are recommended when one is dealing with an excited delirium suspect:

+ An excited delirium suspect should be viewed as a person in a medical crisis. Rescue should be dispatched to the scene and staged in the area for rapid response.

+ *Positional asphyxia* is a condition that can occur when an individual is restrained facedown and is unable to breathe properly. This situation is worsened when pressure is applied (usually with a knee) to the middle and back of the individual's neck. This is why a person's airway needs to be monitored at all times during a restraint. If an individual is restrained facedown, his or her head should be turned to the side. When safety permits, the person should be placed in a sitting position. Someone should always be responsible for securing the head to prevent biting.

+ The less lethal option, *Taser* (Taser International, Inc.) has been helpful in these situations. Have it on hand or call for it to be brought to the scene. Because of the excessive energy and strength in excited delirium, it is not uncommon to need multiple deployments to subdue the person. Once the person is tased and secured, it is recommended to sit the individual up or place him or her on the side to prevent respiratory arrest.

+ Wait for backup before you go hands-on. This is highly recommended because of the excessive strength of an excited delirium suspect. An excited delirium suspect can easily overpower one to two officers.

+ The sooner the individual can receive medication to assist in calming him or her down, the better the outcome. Studies have shown that when rescue personnel can administer medication at the scene, many of the medical complications seen in excited delirium, including sudden death, may be avoided. A medication like ketamine, which is an anesthetic/sedative with rapid onset, produces sedation and tranquility (within three to five minutes) with minimal side effects. Antianxiety medication (Ativan) and antipsychotics (Haldol) are also used. While it is not in the job description of a law enforcement officer to prescribe medication, there is no harm for a well-informed police or corrections officer to ask medical personnel if sedation can be given at the scene.

+ Remember, excited delirium, like a heart attack, is a serious medical condition that could end badly for all if not handled properly.

Attorney William Everett, a former police officer and associate administrator for the league of Minnesota Cities Insurance Trust, stated the following in a *PoliceOne.com* article dated October 14, 2005, concerning excited delirium:

> *Studies estimate that ED may be a factor in 50 to 125 in-custody deaths a year in the United States alone. Part of the problem seems to be that officers' tend to see the bizarre and alarming behavior of a subject experiencing this condition as strictly a control- and- arrest situation rather than as a serious medical emergency that can be fatal. Everett also emphasized the importance of officers learning the difference between a combative intoxicated individual and a person suffering from an untreated medical condition such as diabetes – one goes to jail and the other needs to go to the hospital. (Everett 2005)*

# CHAPTER 4

# CRISIS INTERVENTION TECHNIQUES FOR HANDLING PSYCHOSIS

The following are general guidelines and suggested de-escalating techniques that are effective in assisting mentally ill individuals experiencing psychosis such as in schizophrenia. The good news is that while these basic verbal techniques are effective for individuals experiencing psychosis, they also work well for nonpsychotic individuals experiencing an emotional crisis.

+ Remember, the individual's brain-filtering circuits are malfunctioning, so he or she may *misperceive or misevaluate* your directives and actions.

+ *One officer should do the talking.* A psychotic individual may have trouble focusing and concentrating. Focusing on one voice is easier than trying to focus on multiple speakers. It is also important to limit side conversations, as the person may interpret these conversations as involving him or her.

+ *Remember to keep a safe distance.* Do not compromise safety for rapport. The psychotic individual is most often frightened and may misinterpret your closeness as an attack. Do not touch the individual unless you are going hands-on, as this may precipitate a violent reaction. If a psychotic person bumps into you, easily guide him or her away. Do not physically restrain unless he or she is posing a threat to you or others.

- Call for *less lethal options* to be brought to the scene. A less lethal option such as the *Taser (Taser International, Inc.)* is especially useful with individuals who are psychotic or suicidal. Suicide by cop is a situation in which a suicidal individual attempts to get an officer to shoot him or her. The Taser is highly effective in these situations. Use of OC spray has been known to increase psychotic behavior when used. It has also been implicated in cases of in-custody deaths in which the suspects had asthma (NIJ report 2003).*Try to limit the use of OC spray.* In most cases the suspect becomes more frightened and aggressive after he or she is sprayed.

- *Give the situation time!* Waiting these situations out, as long as violence is not occurring, is much safer for both the officer and the psychotic individuals. Remember, they are usually frightened and need time to understand what you are asking of them.

- *Try to limit noise, sirens, and chaos at the scene.* It is much easier for a person with psychosis to focus if background noise is reduced.

- *Introduce yourself* (with your first name) and try to get the name of the person if possible. For example, you can say, "My name is Ed. I'm a police officer. Can I have your name please?"

- Make it clear to the person that *you are not there to harm* him or her but rather to help. The individual may be paranoid and fearful of you. Make statements such as these: "I am here to help you." "I will keep you safe." "I will help you stay in control and not let anyone harm you."

- If the person appears to be *hallucinating,* attempt to refocus him or her on your voice. Repeat you directive until you get his or her attention. For example, you might say, "I don't want you to listen to any other voice but mine. Listen to my voice. I will not let the voices harm you." Remember, you are trying to get the individual to refocus his or her attention on you, as hallucinations will alter the person's ability to focus on your commands.

- It's important to remember that psychotic individuals may present with *superhuman strength!* This is believed to be caused by large amounts of circulating stress hormones (adrenalin) pouring into their systems at the time of the crises. This is the main reason for avoiding physical restraint and applying control techniques until the individuals have become clear threats to you or others.

- *Use a neutral tone of voice.* Do not raise your voice unless the person is not responding to a neutral voice tone. He or she may be hallucinating.

- If possible tell the person, what you are going to do before you do it. Making quick, abrupt moves can startle psychotic individuals into physical aggression as a self-protective action. Remember, they may misperceive your intentions, so be clear and concise in your communication. Give one direction at a time instead of giving multiple instructions all at once. "John, I will walk with you to the ambulance. I'm going to help you stand."

- Find out if they are on *medication* or if they are in treatment with a mental health provider. This will help you determine whether psychiatric issues exist and where to refer the person if there is no imminent risk.

- *Give clear instructions* and repeat yourself until the person looks at you and responds. You can say, "Sir, I need you to sit down before

I can figure out how to help you." Getting a person suffering from mental illness to sit down gives you valuable information regarding the person's willingness to comply with your directives. Offering structure and direction also helps the person regain the feeling of being in control.

+ *Have rescue or medical personnel stage* near the scene as soon as you identify psychosis or other severe emotional disturbances. It is safer to transport the individual in a rescue as opposed to a squad car. Always transport to a local ER for further evaluation. Avoid taking the psychotic individual back to the station to avoid an in-custody death or medical emergency. It is also important to view all calls involving a mentally ill suspect as being in need of medical intervention in comparison to an arrest and control situation. Treat the call and the person no differently than you would treat a heart attack, stroke, of severe medical trauma victim. This thinking has helped many officers make the right call!

+ If physical restraint is needed, make sure you have enough assistance on hand before you go hands-on if time permits. Make sure that each limb in secured and one officer is assigned the head to prevent biting. Also don't forget to maintain an open airway. Avoid applying direct heavy pressure to the back of the suspect while he or she is in the facedown position to avoid labored breathing and/or asphyxia. Sit the individual up as soon as he or she is secured.

+ Do not act alone! Always have backup available. Sometimes all it takes is a show of force to get an emotionally disturbed person or anyone for that matter to agree to your plan.

+ It is best to not agree with or discount a person's delusional beliefs. For example, if a delusional man feels that his water is poisoned; statements like "Your water is not poisoned" or "I've arrested the terrorist that poisoned the water supply" are not helpful statements. While this may work in the short term, it does nothing for the officer or the department's credibility with this person in the future. Try statements like these: "My job is to keep you safe." "I will not let anyone harm you." "I can see you are scared." "Anyone who believes they are about to die from poison would be scared too." "I will see to it that you get the help you need tonight." If the person is hallucinating, get him or her to focus on your voice. For example, you can say, "Don't listen to the voices. Focus on my voice. I will not let the voices harm you."

And lastly, remember that the psychotic individual or any other person with a chronic mental illness is usually less of a threat to you than the common criminal. The criminal who is not mentally ill is trying to deceive you, lie, or distract you to gain an upper hand. Mentally ill people are confused, frightened, and unable to make sense of the world around them. They need you to guide them to safety and treatment, not incarceration. The good news is that you can still maintain all of your officer safety skills while you follow these guidelines, keeping you, your colleagues and the mentally ill person away from an encounter of deadly force.

# CHAPTER 5

# TASER DEPLOYMENT AND THE MENTALLY ILL

It's important to again mention the use of the Taser (Taser International, Inc.) as a less lethal option. I have personally seen the Taser used to subdue a good number of mentally ill individuals in need of emergency care. The Taser has saved many lives when deployed correctly. That's why having officer's certified in its use is highly recommended.

Unfortunately there have been several cases where a suspects death occured after deployment of the Taser. In most of these cases the suspects were either high on stimulant drugs and/or floridly psychotic at the time they were tased. Individuals in many of these cases were also obese and in poor physical health, and they were involved in physical restraints at the time of their deaths. It is difficult to determine if the Taser played a role in these deaths. We do know that stimulant drugs have been known to cause cardiac arrest in non-obese individuals sitting on their couches, never mind being involved in violent physical encounters with the police. Add obesity and poor health into the mix, and you have an accident waiting to happen with or without Taser deployment. If officers are not supplied with Tasers or other less lethal options like beanbag rounds, they have limited choices to deploy if attacked or faced with a volatile aggressor. We have seen far too many deadly force encounters involving mentally ill individuals in the past. As we know, some deadly force encounters appear unavoidable, as the individual either charged the officer with a bladed weapon, baseball bat, tire iron, or had a firearm ,which caused the officer( as per their training) to use deadly force. If Tasers were on scene during these encounters, outcomes might have been different. I have helped many officers recover and return to work after shootings, and in each of these cases the Taser was either not on scene or available for use. Many departments still do not have Tasers on hand as an option. Having the Taser available for use in these encounters is lifesaving for the mental ill individual as well as the officer who is not forced to shoot the suspect. Many law enforcement administrators are still not offering the Taser for fear of liability issues and lawsuits. As the popularity of the Taser increases, not having it available for officer's use during these encounters may increase as opposed to decrease the potential liability for both the officers and their department.

In 2008 studies conducted by Wake Forest University School of Medicine on the nationwide use of the Taser suggest that the Taser is safe and causes low risk of injuries to both the suspect and the involved officers. Of the thousand cases of Taser use examined by the researchers, 99.7 percent had either no injuries or minor injuries. In a second related study by the Wake Forrest researchers to determine the Taser's effect on cardiac health, twenty-eight police officers underwent one-, three-, and five-second exposures to the Taser. The results were impressive! Normal heart rhythm was recorded before and after each exposure. No cardiac abnormalities were detected. Pulse and blood pressure reading were slightly elevated as expected (no health risk). The researchers conclude that the Taser exposure in both studies appeared to be safe with no increased risk to cardiac health in the population tested. More information on this research can be obtained via the Wake

Forest University Medical Center website. For information regarding in-custody deaths in cases of Taser use, visit the NIJ website at http://www.ncjrs.gov/pdffiles1/nij/222981.pdf.

# CHAPTER 6

# DEPRESSION AND SUICIDE

Individuals who take their own lives are usually suffering from an undiagnosed major depression. Major depression is an emotionally painful and serious medical condition, which if not treated, can result in suicide. Most individuals have experienced occasional feelings of sadness with depressed mood throughout their lives. These episodes of normal depressed mood are usually short-lived and rarely affect a person's ability to function at work or at home. A major depressive disorder is longer-lasting and more intense, and it impairs a person's ability to function. It is experienced most of the day with very little relief. Depression removes all joy and pleasure from a person's life and produces feelings of hopelessness ("I'll never get better"), worthlessness ("I'm useless to my family"), and anxiety. Individuals with a major depression may also have changes in appetite, sleep, energy, and concentration. Suicide ideation and attempts are also seen in depression. When depressed individuals reach points where they no longer want to feel the pain and suffering of depression, they may oftentimes develop thoughts of suicide. Individuals who commit suicide usually do not want to kill themselves. Often they are actively looking for other ways to end the emotional pain and despair caused by depression. If people with depression go untreated or their attempts to find rational solutions to their problems fail, they may turn to their last option—suicide.

It is still unknown what causes a person to develop clinical depression. One current theory is that depression is due to a lack of or underproduction of brain chemicals known as neurotransmitters. Neurotransmitters aid the nerves of the brain (called neurons) to communicate with one another. Brain chemicals believed to play a role in depression are serotonin, norepinephrine, and in some cases dopamine. It is believed that a decrease in one or several of these brain chemicals may cause the symptoms of major depression. Some individuals are believed to have a serotonin deficiency while others appear to have a deficiency of both neurotransmitters. Some men with depression may have a dopamine and norepinephrine deficiency. Serotonin has been labeled the "happy neurotransmitter." When we laugh at a good joke, we believe serotonin is being released in the brain. Serotonin promotes sleep, appetite, relaxation, sex drive, and feelings of self-worth. Norepinephrine is believed to promote energy, alertness, memory, and concentration. It is believed that when these brain chemicals are severely reduced, a person begins to experience the symptoms of depression. Dopamine deficiency may be experienced as a decrease in pleasure and enjoyment, and it is most often accompanied by agitation and behavior disturbances.

We also believe that some people may be more prone to depression than others. We know that individuals with histories of physically or sexually abuse or experience with psychological trauma in early life have higher rates of depression. Depression also runs in families. Having a strong family history of depression places a person at a slightly higher risk, but that does not mean the individual will develop depression. Individuals who socially isolate, lack social and spiritual supports, and are unemployed are also at a higher risk. While we believe depression may have a chemical component, it is also known that a person's general outlook on life and how he or she copes with daily stress and adversity may hold the key to why some get it and some don't. While researchers are not sure if having a positive outlook or a "glass half full" mind-set in approaching daily life can reduce a person's chance of getting depression, it certainly can't hurt! Most of us remember the sadness felt after losing a loved one or the emotional hurt experienced after a major breakup. While these events upset us, we were still able to carry on with our daily responsibilities—working, paying the bills, showering, and shopping. Maybe we took several personal days from work and hung around in our pajamas and watched TV, but eventually we shook off the sadness and returned to our daily routine. Individuals who are clinically depressed cannot shake off the sadness, and as each day goes by, the pain and suffering of depression lives on.

The latest edition of the *Diagnostic and Statistical Manual of Psychiatry* (DSM-V) is considered the bible of psychiatry. All known psychiatric illnesses along with a listing of the history, characteristics, and signs and symptoms of each psychiatric disorder are listed. To be diagnosed with major depression, an individual has to experience five depressive symptoms for at least a two-week period (duration) with a significant decrease in daily functioning (intensity). At least one of the five symptoms needs to be either a significant change in mood or a loss of interest and pleasure in an individual's usual activities. The clinically depressed person experiences symptoms of depression for most or all of the day with very little relief experienced. It is hypothesized that once serotonin and possibly other brain chemical levels fall in the brain, an individual begins to experience the symptoms of depression—decreased sleep, nightmares, poor concentration, memory loss, hopelessness, worthlessness, physical pain (headache, stomachache, backache, etc.), loss of interest, loss of pleasure, loss of libido, tearfulness, anxiety, irritability, decreased energy, and possibly suicide ideation. Remember, an individual needs to have at least five symptoms to warrant a diagnosis of major depression. While having two or three of the above symptoms may be problematic for most, it is still not indicative of a major depressive episode until the individual has experienced at least five. When it is determined that an individual is suffering from major depression, treatment should consist of both antidepressant medication and counseling. Hospitalization is only warranted for individuals who are acutely suicidal. Most individuals can be seen on an outpatient basis. Outpatient treatment usually consists of weekly individual sessions, family involvement (if appropriate), and regularly scheduled visits with a psychiatrist for medication monitoring. Antidepressants, such as Prozac, Celexa, Lexapro Paxil, or Zoloft, known as selective serotonin reuptake inhibitors or SSRIs, may be prescribed. These medications are selective for serotonin, which means they only raise the levels of serotonin in the brain. SSRIs are usually the first drugs prescribed for major depression, as they have slightly less side effects than older antidepressants, such as Elavil or Imipramine. SSRIs, when taken alone, are not lethal in an overdose. It is also believed that a good number of individuals with depression only suffer from a serotonin deficiency, making SSRIs the first drugs of choice. Older medications, such as Elavil and Desipramine, known as tricyclics, can be lethal in an overdose. This is a major reason why newer antidepressants are preferred to the old.

If SSRIs are not effective in lifting a person's depression, there are other antidepressants available. These medications are known as dual-action antidepressants and include Remeron, Effexor, and Cymbalta. They are believed to work by increasing several neurotransmitters in the brain as opposed to only one as with SSRIs. Most dual-action agents raise both serotonin and norepinephrine. They are also not lethal in overdose like SSRIs, so if a single-action agent like Paxil, which works on serotonin only, does not work, the doctor may prescribe a dual-action agent like Cymbalta, which increases both serotonin and norepinephrine. Wellbutrin is an antidepressant that seems to work particularly well in men. It is believed to increase dopamine and norepinephrine. The good news is that if one antidepressant does not work, there are many others available to treat depression. It is important to know that antidepressants do not work quickly. They may take on average up to four to six weeks to work. Here's a word of caution regarding antidepressants: Antidepressants are known as "activating drugs," especially in the first week or two of treatment. In other words, they only improve what is called objective (what others see) signs and symptoms like energy, sleep, and appetite disturbances. Subjective symptoms of improvement like feelings of self-worth, optimism, hope, enjoyment, and increased mood usually occur anywhere from two to eight weeks out. If a depressed individual was asked how he or she felt during the first week of treatment, the person would most likely not offer a positive response. Remember, an individual may look better to you (objective) but still feel deeply depressed (subjective). What can be dangerous during the first several weeks of treatment prior to subjective improvement is the fact that the risk of suicide remains high. If an individual has suicide ideation but does not have the energy to plan and commit suicide, taking an antidepressant may precipitate a suicide attempt because of the drug's activating or energizing properties. Despite this, the benefits of taking antidepressants far exceed the risks. If an individual does not receive treatment with antidepressants, his or her suicide risk substantially increases. Antidepressants also effectively treat many of the symptoms of PTSD, such as sleep disturbance, irritability, intrusive thoughts, depressed moods, and anxiety.

Older medications to treat depression still work well to lift depression but are used less today do to their lethality if taken in an overdose. If you see an empty bottle of these medications medical assistance should be accessed asap! It is also important to again note that most of the newer antidepressants can also be used to treat anxiety and post traumatic stress disorder. Here is a short list of the most common older medications:

- Amitriptyline ( Elavil)
- Sinequan ( Doxepin)
- Imipramine ( Norpramin)

Newer medications with a lower risk of overdose lethality (if taken alone) are as follows:

- Fluoxitine ( Prozac)
- Paroxitine ( Paxil)
- Sertraline ( Zoloft)
- Escitalopram ( Lexapro)
- Citalopram ( Celexa)
- Fluvoxamine ( Luvox)
- Duloxetine ( Cymbalta)
- Venlafaxine ( Effexor)
- Bupropion ( Wellbutrin/ Zyban)
- Mirtazapine ( Remeron )
- Trazdone ( mostly used for sleep)

When a depressed individual who is on antidepressants makes statements such as "I think I'm going to get through this" or "I feel better," that person is on his or her way to recovery. Sometimes an individual may present a sudden change in mood and appear happier and content. This may seem promising on the surface, but it may also be a clue to an impending suicide attempt. If a depressed individual has made up his or her mind to commit suicide, that person may seem as happy, optimistic, and content before he or she attempts suicide. The person may view suicide as the only solution to end suffering and pain. Watch out for times when individuals either begin putting their affairs in order or giving away treasured belongings. I once evaluated a man with depression who impulsively gave away his motorcycle to a friend. Luckily a family member identified this act as a warning sign of impending suicide and obtained immediate help for the person. It is well known that most individuals who commit suicide share their thoughts with friends or family members before their deaths. Talking about suicide is a cry for help. Dismissing these statements as harmless could cost an individual his or her life! That is not to say that one person is responsible for the suicide of another, but every effort should be made to intervene if warning signs are seen. It is not normal to joke about committing suicide. This again is another warning cry for help that must not be overlooked.

Men and women may present differently when they are depressed. It is more common for women to present with tearfulness and sadness while men present with irritability, anger, and aggression. Women also have three times greater the risk of developing depression than men. It is my belief that many men go undiagnosed, as they are usually more reluctant to seek help than women are.

While this book is written to help law enforcement officers recognize and respond to mentally ill individuals in crisis, there are high rates of depression and suicide with both police and correction officers. Male law enforcement officers are especially reluctant to seek out help for their depression because of the fear of being stigmatized by their peers. Concerns over being labeled as "crazy" or "unfit for duty" are prevalent among depressed uniformed personnel in law enforcement. So while it is important to be able to recognize depression in individuals you come in contact with while performing your duties, it is also important to be able to recognize the signs in fellow officers.

The following is an actual case example that illustrates the course of major depression in a police officer. The events have been changed to protect confidentiality. One evening a thirty-five-year-old, ten-year-veteran police officer, while in his or her cruiser, noticed a young child playing near the edge of a river on the outskirts of town. As the officer was about to stop their vehicle, he/she lost sight of the child. Fearing the worst, the officer rushed to the water's edge but still could not see or hear the child. While he or she was radioing for assistance, the officer could hear faint screams for help and saw what he believed to be a child trying to stay afloat about thirty feet from shore. The river had a strong undercurrent, and the officer knew that a small child could not survive in the water for long. Disregarding his or her safety, the officer jumped in to the river and swam toward the child but again lost sight of the boy. The officer dove underwater several times, but despite his or her heroic efforts, could not find the child. Shaken, cold, exhausted, and emotionally numb, the officer was assisted out of the water by rescue personnel who arrived on the scene. As rescuers continued to search the river for the missing child, the officer sat at the river's edge, praying that the child would be safely found. Moments later the child's lifeless body was pulled from the river. EMTs initiated CPR, but to no avail. The child had died at the scene. The officer sat speechless as department detectives attempted to gather details and information regarding the incident.

The officer gave their statement to detectives on scene, and subsequently was sent home to his/her spouse and two children. During the next several days the officer expressed normal sadness regarding the child's death. The officer returned to work but did not appear to be their usual self. It became evident to colleagues at work that the officer was blaming thenselves for the death of the child.

During a four-week period after the event the officer's spouse noticed a change in his or her personality. The officer became distant, preferring to isolate as opposed to engaging in family activities. He/she began to experience decreased sleep with early morning awakenings, and found it difficult to return to sleep due to experiencing nightmares. One recurring nightmare found the officer back in the lake, unable to respond to the boy's cries for help. The officer's energy also dropped significantly, and they experienced anxiety attacks at work for no apparent reason. The officer lost interest and pleasure in usual activities as well as demonstrated by his/her refusal to play catch with his/her children, an activity they had previously enjoyed together. The officer canceled a long-awaited trip with friends and dropped out of the department's softball team. Other symptoms experienced included a loss of appetite, fifteen-pound weight loss, increased irritability, hopelessness, a feeling of low self-worth, and a distinct change in mood. He or she was tormented by intrusive thoughts of the drowning and turned to alcohol to suppress these thoughts. The officer soon began to have fleeting thoughts of suicide, thinking that their family would be better off without them. The officer saw him or herself as a burden.

At this point, if the officer had not received immediate care and treatment for his/her symptoms of depression and PTSD, he/she may have attempted suicide. Many times PTSD and depression occur simultaneously, and it can be difficult to diagnose which disorder a person is suffering from. The officer was fortunate that their department had a peer support team. One of the team members reached out to the officer at their home and convinced him/her to see one of the team's mental health professionals. After two sessions with the mental health professional, he/she agreed to see the mental health team psychiatrist, who prescribed antidepressant medication. The officer was diagnosed with major depression and post-traumatic stress disorder. The officer began seeing one of the team's licensed social workers for individual and family counseling. An important part of the counseling process is providing education to both the officer and his significant other about major depression, PTSD, and antidepressant medication. Helping both the officer and his significant other understand the signs and symptoms, duration, and treatment of depression is a major focus of the first two sessions. Early on in treatment, helping the individual and his or her family members understand that there is hope for recovery, and that they are "not alone" in battling this medical illness, is a key component of the counseling approach. It's important to emphasize that the officer's symptoms are medically based and that they are not due to an emotional weakness. Both the officer and their significant other also receive education on the expected action of antidepressants and the need to closely monitor the officer over the first few weeks of treatment because of the activating properties of the medication. (It may increase the risk of suicide.) The counselor also reminded them that subjective improvement, which is seen as a return of hope, optimism, interest, pleasure, and enjoyment in activities, is an important sign of improvement and more important than the officer objectively looking better.

After three weeks of treatment the officer began to feel like his/her old self again. Sleep, appetite, and energy levels returned to normal, and the officer began to experience interest and pleasure in daily activities once again. The officer was more hopeful for the future, and he/she experienced a reduction in both anxiety and intrusive thoughts of the traumatic event. The officer eventually returned to baseline functioning (predepressive state) and returned to work happier, healthier, and more optimistic for the future. He/she will still need to continue treatment for PTSD until he/she fully recovers from the traumatic event. As illustrated by this case example, having trained police peer support officers and mental health professionals available for law enforcement officers experiencing emotional distress can, simply put, save lives. While this case example involved a police officer, many of the depressive symptoms experienced by this individual are often seen in both civilians and military veterans suffering from major depression and/or PTSD, which we will cover in the next chapter.

# CHAPTER 7

# DEPRESSION AND PTSD IN MILITARY PERSONNEL

Why is it important to know when you're dealing with a military veteran when responding to a call for assistance? Most military veterans are skilled in using firearms and have basic or advanced training in self-defense. This makes them a bit more dangerous than the general public when they suffer emotional crises. The good news is that the majority of military veterans returning from combat do not develop depression or PTSD. Most veterans face a normal six- to eight-week period of adjustment from life in a combat zone to civilian life back in the states. Most will acclimate back into society with little difficulty and have much to offer their communities and future employers. For some, conditions like PTSD and depression will go untreated, posing a threat to the veterans, their families, or law enforcement officers responding to crisis calls in the community. Veterans from past military conflicts such as Vietnam may also come in contact with the criminal justice system. We also know that alcohol and drug use is common in veterans experiencing PTSD and/or depression. As mentioned earlier, alcohol, depression, and PTSD do not mix well. If a veteran in crisis is depressed, is drinking heavily, and has firearms in their possession, you must approach with extreme caution. The suicide rate for returning veterans from Iraq and Afghanistan is also high. Firearms have been used in the majority of suicides in the veteran population. Some veterans with PTSD will experience flashbacks, hallucinations, and a situation called dissociation. Dissociation is a situation where veterans can become confused regarding their surroundings and feel like they are back in combat. They may walk the perimeter of their homes with firearms, become combative, and express paranoid thoughts. They are often arrested and incarcerated for violence, which is also common with depression and PTSD. They may get involved in auto accidents or fights and commit crimes as a type of self-punishment or displaced anger. Before discussing this next case, it is important to keep in mind that most military veterans do not have histories of violence toward others and are responsible gun owners. The majority of veteran's with depression and/or PTSD are also not prone to gun violence. We do know that for those untreated veterans with PTSD and/or depression, there are higher rates of violence and suicide.

In January 2013, an Iraq war veteran with an alleged diagnosis of PTSD shot and killed two fellow veterans who were providing him support. One of the veteran's killed was Chris Kyle, the author of the best-selling book *American Sniper*. Kyle was a highly decorated war veteran who spent a good amount of his postmilitary career helping troubled veterans. It appears that Kyle and a fellow veteran took the individual to a firing range to assist him in coping with existing life stressors. Media reports list the following information regarding the shooter's behaviors prior to the incident:

+ He demonstrated anger with his father prior to the shooting because his father wanted to sell his gun.

- He left the house and threatened to "blow his brains out" six months before the incident. He was placed in protective custody at that time by police and transported to a hospital for psychiatric evaluation.

- He spent several years in and out of various VA treatment facilities for PTSD.

- After the shooting he was placed on suicide watch while he was in prison

- He presented after the shooting with aggression while he was incarcerated. In one incident he refused to give up a fork and meal tray, requiring CO intervention.

- He did not take his own life at the scene.

- He drove Kyle's vehicle to a family residence where he confessed to the crime. When police arrived, he appeared intoxicated but went voluntarily with police without a struggle.

It is possible that this individual was suffering from either depression, PTSD, or a combination of both disorders. As mentioned in the chapter on suicide and depression, it is common for men to present with symptoms of aggression, irritability, violence, suicidal thoughts, and impaired judgment when they are depressed. These symptoms are also common in PTSD, which is one reason these disorders are treated simultaneously with both antidepressants and antianxiety medications.

What should law enforcement officers do when they are faced with a distressed veteran?

Again, you should follow your training instincts but keep in mind that the veteran may be misinterpreting or misperceiving your actions as a threat to his or her life. While this is not the psychosis of schizophrenia, the same techniques are used. The following guidelines should help when you are faced with a distressed veteran or depressed individual:

- Try to obtain knowledge of the possession of firearms and of the person's combat experience. It is also important to obtain information regarding past police and/or family reports of violence if available.

- Identifying yourself as a law enforcement officer who is there to help (using your first name) is a start. You can also ask for the person's name.

- If these individual look dazed or confused, orient them to their surroundings. "John, you are in your yard with your wife and kids, not in Iraq." "No one is going to hurt you. You are safe." "I am a police officer, not an insurgent." "John, you are in prison. I am a CO with no intent to harm you." Ask them for the names of their wives and children to remind them that they have others who love them.

- The veteran will be more unpredictable if intoxicated. Have the Taser on hand or enough officers to safely go hands-on before you act. If there is no firearm or high risk to others, you have time!

- If you are in a negotiator's role or are the only officer, *listen closely* to what they are saying. For example, saying, "If that situation happened to me, I would be upset too," shows your attempt to understand. Don't say, "I understand," as you don't. Others things you can say to gain trust and show empathy are as follows: "I can see you are suffering with this." "You're not alone." "Lots of people get depressed and eventually get better." "I will see to it that you get the help you need." "You will get better!" Showing confidence helps the individual see you as a leader. *You should also thank them for their service and sacrifice.*

- It is important to try to place yourself in their shoes. If they are depressed, you are trying to instill hope ("You can get better"), reduce paranoia ("I'm here to help, not harm") and attempt to understand by listening ("If I had seen or experienced that, I or anyone would be just as upset").

Developing a contact at the local veteran's center, VA, or justice assistance program for veterans in your area is a good idea. The military is also addressing issues of depression and PTSD in its personnel stationed in Iraq and Afghanistan. Combat stress teams are available in the field to assist troops in dealing with the stresses of combat. Small teams of military-trained mental health workers and psychologists are available for troops in need of psychological support. Back in the United States, groups of mental health professionals in the private sector are joining forces to provide services for returning veterans and their family members. Groups like Strategic Outreach to Families of All Reservist or SOFAR (www.sofarusa.org) provide services for reservists and their family members. As part of this program, family readiness groups, which are made up of volunteer trauma-trained professionals, are available to help families deal with the stressors of deployment. Outpatient clinics, called veteran centers, are located throughout the United States and provide counseling and also support to returning veterans. Staffed by trained counselors and veteran peer supporters, Veteran's centers offer trauma, substance abuse, marital and family, employment, and educational services for returning veterans. The *Wounded Warrior Project* is also an excellent resource for returning veterans with combat related physical or psychological injuries. They can be reached by phone at 904-296-7350, or at WoundedWarriorProject.org. To contact a veteran center, or other support service, or for more information on combat-related depression and PTSD, visit the following websites: http://www.vetcenter.va.gov, http://www.va.gov, http://www.militaryonesource.com, and http://www.ncptsd.va.gov.

# CHAPTER 8

# SUICIDE BY COP

Suicide by cop is a term used to describe a person who forces a law enforcement officer into using deadly force as a way to commit suicide. Common scenarios include an individual who is depressed and lunges at an officer with a baseball bat, tire iron, or bladed weapon. The individual may also point a loaded (or unloaded) gun at law enforcement officers in an attempt to get them to fire their weapon. Most often the person has suicidal intent but is unable to follow through themselves. These people seek out law enforcement officers to help them commit suicide, understanding that officers will use deadly force when their lives or the lives of others are at risk. This type of deadly force incident seems to produce more post-incident aftershocks for involved officers once they discover that the suspects were emotionally disturbed and suicidal as opposed to criminals trying to escape.

How does an officer recognize a suicide-by-cop situation? This is a hard one to answer, as you need to follow your instincts. Be aware that in most of these situations alcohol is involved. People will do things under the influence that they would never do when sober. Alcohol shuts off an important part of the human brain called the prefrontal cortex. The prefrontal cortex is responsible for giving a person rational thought and judgment. Shut down the prefrontal cortex, and all judgment goes "out the window." This may also explain why people say things they later regret and act in ways that are not the norm when they are intoxicated. Alcohol is also a depressant, which means it depresses brain activity and increases depressed mood. If the person is depressed prior to drinking, the effect of alcohol usually intensifies the depression.

In many cases of suicide by cop as well as suicide in general, a recent breakup in a significant relationship is a high risk factor for attempting suicide. We also know that being diagnosed with a life-threatening illness can also precipitate a suicidal act. It is also believed that some men (as most cases of this act are men) feel that going to their death in a shootout is a macho way to go, possibly reducing the stigma attached to committing suicide (i.e., people saying, "He was weak."). Another common factor is the person *asking to be killed*. Most criminals do not ask for death. Remember, individuals who are depressed are in emotional pain. They feel that death is a better option than facing another day with depression. They see their situations as hopeless, and you are the answer to their problems. The Taser can be deployed in these situations when bladed weapons or other blunt objects like tire irons are used by suspects. Again, a tire iron can be just as dangerous as a firearm, so follow your officer safety instincts.

Feeling justified in using deadly force is a big emotional hurdle an officer must achieve before he or she is able to return to work. Feeling justified in killing a bad guy is easier to accept than killing an emotionally disturbed person. The officer can recover; it's just is a bit harder.

# CHAPTER 9
# SUICIDE AWARENESS TIPS

One of the first steps in preventing suicide is knowing what to look for in a person presenting in emotional distress. All individuals who express suicidal thinking should be evaluated by a mental health professional. Remember, the individual may deny having thoughts of suicide in your presence. If the person's family reports suicidal statements or the person has demonstrated behaviors listed below, it may be best to access an evaluation—better to be safe than sorry.

The following behaviors have been noted in depressed individuals who also have suicide ideation:

- Change in personality or mood—The person may become sad, easily angered, withdrawn, irritable, anxious, agitated, or tired. The loss of facial expression or a state of not smiling may occur in depression.
- Content of speech—The person may talk about committing suicide or wanting to die. He or she may appear preoccupied with death and dying. You may notice a reduction in talking to others. The individual may express feelings of worthlessness and say, "I'm a failure"

- Expressed hopelessness—The person may voice no hope for the future and may make statements like, "I will never get better."

- Change in behavior—An inability to concentrate on school, work and routine tasks are common. The person may be overly tearful or sad for most of the day. He or she may have more difficulty functioning in the morning and may present as irritable and angry with others.

- Change in sleep pattern—Oversleeping, insomnia, nightmares, and waking up early in a cold sweat are common.

- Change in eating habits—You may notice unusual weight loss or gain. It's more common to see loss of appetite. You may see complaints of upset stomach or difficulty swallowing.

- Loss of religion—The person may lose faith in God or stop going to church. The individual may also feel that he or she is being punished for sins committed.

- Drug or alcohol use—There may be a noted increase in the use of drugs or alcohol. The person may be using substances as a way of medicating their symptoms of anxiety or depression.

- High-risk behaviors—The person may be driving fast, getting into car accidents, using drugs, gambling, fighting, and/or having promiscuous sex.

- Giving away possessions—A person sometimes prepares for death by giving away possessions or treasured belongings.

- Putting affairs in order—The person may make out a will, pay bills far in advance of due date, or take out an insurance policy.

- Self-blame or hatred—The person may express worthlessness, guilt, or shame. The individual may make statements that indicate that he or she sees him or herself as a burden to the family.

+ Recent losses—The person may have suffered a loss of a job, status, relationship, physical health, divorce, or the death of a loved one.

+ Suicidal actions—The person may be cutting his or her wrists, taking pills, and making suicidal statements. Watch for increased involvement in auto accidents or violent acts.

+ Individual or family history of prior suicide attempts—This places a person at a higher risk of committing suicide in the future.

+ Access to a firearm in the home—If a depressed person has access to a firearm, he or she is more apt to use it!

It is common for individuals who commit suicide to either have spoken to someone about their thoughts or given some kind of clue or warning sign prior to the act of suicide. It is important not to ignore suicidal threats or gestures. For example, statements such as "You would be better off without me" or "I'm better off dead" may indicate suicidal intent. A sudden lift in mood may also be a warning sign. This may imply that the person is at peace with his or her decision to commit suicide. It's important to know that people contemplating suicide are often ambivalent. Even the most severely depressed person has mixed feelings about death. It is never too late to intervene with a suicidal person. Offering hope, encouragement, and timely assistance can (and in most cases will) give a depressed person hope for recovery by ending his or her thoughts of suicide.

While most law enforcement agencies have trained negotiators available to take the lead in situations involving depressed and suicidal individuals, negotiators may not be available for some time, requiring officers first on the scene to begin verbal negotiations.

The following tips and communication strategies are suggested when one is attempting to de-escalate a depressed individual who may be contemplating suicide. While several of these techniques were mentioned in earlier chapters, they are listed again with slight modifications to address depression.

Remember, maintaining officer safety, such as keeping a safe distance while communicating, should be maintained throughout all crisis situations. It is also important to remember that no technique is foolproof and individuals may still kill themselves despite your efforts. What you say will in no way make these people kill themselves. They have most often made up their minds that suicide is their only option. But as we said earlier, suicidal thoughts wax and wane, and the goal of using these techniques is to get the individuals, through understanding, to rethink or eliminate suicide as a solution to their problem.

1. *Establish verbal contact* by asking the name of the individual and by introducing yourself (using your first name). Proceed to explain that you are there to help. "John, I'm here to help. How can I help you today?"

2. *Listen for expressed hopelessness.* Depressed individuals oftentimes will express thoughts that their situations can only get worse. This symptom of depression is called hopelessness. Offering hope that the person can get better is a technique that can sometimes lessen hopelessness. This can be achieved with statements such as, "John, you can get better, and I will see to it that you get the help you need."

3. Individuals with depression are also *unable to make rational decisions* about what to do to get better. They most often need someone who, with confidence, can lead them to safety. Officers are in a great position to provide the leadership and guidance

needed by using statements such as the following: "John, I will make sure you get the help you need." "If you do what I tell you tonight, you will get better." "I will not let you hurt yourself. Put the knife down."

4. It is also common for individuals with depression to believe that they are *alone in their suffering*. Statements such as, "John, I have spoken with and helped many people with depression, and they all feel as you do. You are not alone in feeling this way." Statements that show your understanding of depression will help demonstrate to these people that they are not alone with experiencing depression and that others have suffered as they have. Showing an understanding of depression will also make officers more credible in the eyes of these people, which improves the chances of a positive outcome.

5. *Listen to the content of what they are saying.* Giving depressed individuals time in expressing concerns, if immediate safety is not a concern, will give officers a chance to normalize the thoughts and feelings expressed by these people. This is the "putting yourself in their shoes" technique. You could say, "John, if my wife and kids left in the middle of the night, it would upset me too." Or you could say, "If I lost my job and felt as sad as you do, I might be thinking the same way." Again, this technique is very effective is both showing understanding for the person's concerns and normalizing, demonstrating that most folks would feel the same way if placed in a similar situation.

6. ·Continue to repeat instructions. Depressed individuals, as in psychosis, may not be processing information correctly. So repeating your commands (without anger) increases the chances of the individuals understanding what you want them to do.

7. Most suicidal and depressed individuals *do not want to kill themselves.* They are thinking of suicide to end the emotional pain they are experiencing. "John, I know you feel that this is the only way to end the pain you are experiencing. My job tonight is to help you believe that there is another way."

8. *Utilize the Taser* or other less lethal options if these individuals have bladed weapons or they are actively self-abusive.

# CHAPTER 10

# BIPOLAR DISORDER

Bipolar disorder, also known as manic depressive illness, is a severe and persistent mental illness like schizophrenia that runs in families. In order to have bipolar disorder, a person has to have what is called a manic episode along with one episode of depression. A manic episode is the opposite of depression. The person presents with excessive energy as opposed to decreased energy as seen in depression. Many times the person in a manic phrase of bipolar disorder has an inflated self-esteem. These people may believe they can fly, work as a secret agent, or can change the weather. They also talk rapidly and are either extremely happy or irritable. Mania can also cause a person to dress in vivid colors, and women have been known to wear excessive makeup. People with bipolar disorder may be found on the street or in their cells, preaching the Bible. They may also be found recklessly running barefoot in the park or may be picked up by police after they have walked many miles from home with no destination. They also spend money excessively and can be sexually promiscuous. These manic episodes usually last seven to ten days and usually end up with the person being hospitalized because of the extreme nature of his or her behavior. Individuals also have periods of depression mixed in with episodes of mania. The depression looks identical to the depression explained previously.

Experts are not sure what causes bipolar disorder. While having a family history of bipolar disorder places a person at greater risk of developing this disorder, it does not mean that the individual will develop the disorder. We believe the same chemicals that are reduced in depression may be increased in mania, which could explain the increased activity as opposed to the decrease seen in depression. Remember, stimulant drugs can cause a maniclike syndrome. If toxicology results are positive for cocaine, amphetamines, or PCP, the behavior is most likely due to drug use. Bath salts can also cause manic and psychotic symptoms. If the manic behavior was due to the person taking illicit drugs, the symptoms should abate in twenty-four to forty-eight hours. If the manic behavior was due to a mental illness, it usually takes several weeks for the person to fully recover.

Medications are used to reduce the manic and depressive episodes seen in bipolar. Medications like lithium, Depakote, Tegretol, and antipsychotics are used. Antipsychotics are the same medicines used for schizophrenia. Antipsychotics are used to sedate and reduce the symptoms of mania. If individuals with bipolar disorder take their medication, they usually do well. The problem again is with a person's insight or ability to understand the need to take medications. Most individuals with bipolar disorder do not like taking medications. Medications for bipolar disorder eliminate the natural high feeling of mania, which is an enjoyable feeling for most.

As I previously stated, most individuals with bipolar mania need to be hospitalized for their own safety. One approach used to get the person with mania into an ambulance is to have an officer of the opposite sex of the person do the talking. Because individuals with mania may experience the symptoms of hypersexuality and appear highly flirtatious, an officer from the opposite sex will usually have better compliance results. I have seen this approach work many times. All of the interventions recommended for the individual with psychosis are usually effective for the person presenting with bipolar disorder.

# CHAPTER 11

# PERSONALITY DISORDERS

Law enforcement officers, whether working in a correction facility or patrolling streets, run into individuals with problematic behaviors on a daily basis while they are performing their duties. Many of these individuals have what are called personality disorders. We all have personality traits. Personality traits make us who we are. Some individuals have trouble with controlling anger and hostility or tend to be shy and passive, while others are overdramatic and attention-seeking. Some have obsessive-compulsive traits. They want their world neat, orderly, and controlled. One example of this is a person who uses and depends on a daily list to organize and accomplish tasks throughout the day or one who likes to keep his or her belongings neat and organized in certain spots within the home. Others have what are called dependent traits, which manifest as difficulties with making decisions or letting go of relationships. Some have what are called histrionic traits, which mean they have a strong need to be the center of attention and tend to be loud and melodramatic. Others have what are known as narcissistic traits, and they believe they are smarter, more attractive, or superior to other people. Some folks prefer to be alone and never marry, while others are in and out of relationships like the wind.

All of the above examples of personality traits are normal (you can relax!) and make us who we are. If these personality traits become long-standing or problematic and interfere with a person's ability to function at home and at work, a personality disorder is most often present. It is not uncommon for a person with a personality disorder to have difficulty controlling anger, managing stress, and getting along with others. Individuals with personality disorders are also more apt to get involved in both verbal and physical confrontations with others. They also are more often arrested for domestic violence, assault and battery, breaking and entering, sexual assault, and disorderly conduct than individuals with major mental illnesses, such as schizophrenia and bipolar disorder as mentioned earlier. You may also see compulsive lying and deception, and these people are often described as being cold and uncaring in relationships. The interpersonal and family difficulties experienced by someone with a personality disorder are often carried over into a workplace setting. Individuals with personality disorders usually have trouble following rules and taking orders from authority, which often translates into multiple firing or employment changes.

The following are some common behavior's seen in individuals with personality disorders:

+ chronic suicide ideation
+ self-abuse (cutting, burning, head banging, etc.)
+ substance abuse
+ multiple arrests for assault and battery
+ chronic lying and stealing
+ trouble controlling anger
+ superficial cutting on arms, legs, wrist, and forearms.
+ history of physical and/or sexual abuse in childhood
+ having rapid changes in mood often ( from happy to sad)

- stormy relationships
- trouble holding down jobs
- perpetrator of domestic violence
- trouble with authority
- chronic fighting and chaotic lifestyle
- a lack of involvement from family and friends
- attention-seeking behavior (fainting, yelling, loud, demanding, etc.)
- overdramatic and overly flirtatious
- on multiple medications with very little effect

The following information is a brief description of two of the more problematic personality disorders called borderline personality disorder and antisocial personality disorder.

## Borderline Personality

Borderline personality disorder is seen more often in women than in men. It is one of the most disabling personality disorders, which experts believe may develop in early childhood. When we explore the developmental backgrounds of women with this disorder, we find significant histories of childhood physical and sexual abuse. Individuals with borderline personality disorder have difficulty establishing trusting relationships with others. It is believed that this mistrust develops in children because of repeated physical and/or sexual abuse perpetrated on them. Children should be able to trust that their parents will keep them safe from harm. Experiencing repeated sexual abuse at the hand of relatives can and will destroy children's sense of safety and trust. Being a victim of child abuse can also cause much confusion about personal boundaries in relationships with others. Personal boundaries tell us how to react in social situations—how close to stand next to a stranger, how much personal information to give out to someone we don't know, and when and with whom a person decides to have sexual relations. It is believed that these difficulties are again due to the effects of being sexually abused by a loved one. Children need to trust in a caregiver's ability to teach them right from wrong, protect them from harm, and teach them the importance of trust. Therefore, if these children do not receive immediate and ongoing help and protection from further harm, they will carry these issues into adulthood. This is one reason we see a large number of women with this disorder involved in prostitution, substance abuse, and/or exotic dancing.

Individuals with borderline personality use self-abuse, such as superficially cutting their wrists and forearms, to feel relief. It is believed that this self-cutting behavior can become addicting because of the natural release of the body's own painkilling substances called endorphins. Self-abuse appears to relieve the emotional anesthesia as well as numbing and trancelike states called dissociation, which are experienced prior to the self-abusive episodes. When under highly stressful situations in adulthood, the person experiences this emotional anesthesia and turns to self-abuse to bring him or her back into reality. This is why we believe that a person with borderline personality will say that he or she feels better after cutting.

Individuals with this disorder also have chronic thoughts of suicide and self-harm. They are frequently seen in local emergency rooms and by police and rescue on emergency runs because of suicidal thoughts or attempts. Depressed mood, low self-esteem, and hopelessness are also present. They also have the tendency to see people in the world as either good or evil.

The following case example should illustrate this good vs. evil dichotomy.

A male police officer responds to a call for assistance because of an alleged suicide attempt. When the officer arrives, he discovers a twenty-five-year-old female sitting on the sidewalk in front of her apartment. She states she did a stupid thing by cutting her wrist after getting in a disagreement with her boyfriend. She states she is not currently suicidal. She then proceeds to tell the officer that he is the kindest and most understanding police officer she has ever met (good). The individual then proceeds to disclose detailed personal information to the officer, which is an indicator of poor personal boundaries. Most folks don't disclose this type of information to strangers. Over the next several days the individual leaves multiple phone messages for the officer at the station and also sends him a letter. In the letter she asks if she can meet the officer for coffee. When the officer returns her call and explains that he can't meet her for coffee, she becomes angry, yelling and screaming on the phone that "all men are alike" (evil). The officer went from a position of being the best to the worst in a moment's notice. As you can see from this example, rapid and unpredictable behavior is common in this disorder.

Unfortunately there are no medicines that can fix or cure an individual with borderline personality. It is important to realize that this is a lifelong pattern of emotional instability, self-abuse, and problems getting along with others. They often have few friends and severely strained relationships with family members. Medications are used to help with depressed moods (antidepressants), explosiveness, and self-abuse.

Counseling and case management services provided by a community-based mental health center (CMHC) is the preferred treatment setting for someone with this disorder. These agencies provide MDs, RNs, and counselors that can provide intensive community-based services when needed. Medications, if warranted, target symptoms of self-abuse, impulse control, anger, and depression. It is not uncommon to see a person with this disorder on many psychiatric medications because of the reoccurring moods swings and anger/impulse control issues (fighting, breaking objects, etc.) seen in this disorder. Oftentimes medications are added when symptoms worsen or the current medications prescribed are not working. Medications are also not withdrawn once the episode is over. As stated earlier, many individuals don't respond to medication, as we are dealing with a lifelong disorder of personality as opposed to a progressive medical/psychiatric illness like schizophrenia or bipolar disorder. In other words, medications can effectively work in reducing symptoms like hallucinations, delusions, mania, and major depression in a person with a severe and persistent mental illness, but the same approach may not and oftentimes does not work with an individual with borderline personality. So individuals end up on multiple medications, which increase their suicide risk. Since these individuals attempt or threaten suicide, often it is preferred that they are on as little medication as possible.

It is also common for individuals with borderline and other personality disorders to abuse substances. The person often turns to substances that sedate and produce a tranquil effect, such as alcohol, opiates, and marijuana. All of these drugs produce a calming effect, reducing the irritability, rage, anger, and emotional instability seen in a person with a personality disorder.

## Antisocial Personality Disorder

Antisocial personality disorder, also known as the criminal personality or the sociopath, poses the most risk to the safety of a law enforcement officer. Individuals with this disorder believe that societal laws do not apply to them. They chronically lie, steal, cheat, fight, and manipulate others as a way of life. They understand the consequences of their actions but simply do not care. They purposely violate the law for personal gain. Individuals with this disorder are often seen as cunning, charming, and manipulative. They also have no regard for human life, which is one reason this population will kill, hurt and attack others without consciousness. Individuals with this diagnosis are the most dangerous people in society. They show little remorse for their actions. If people with this disorder are arrested, they may appear emotionally upset upon arrest, not because of what they did but rather because they were caught committing their crimes. This diagnosis is commonly seen in rapists, murderers, serial killers, gang members, pedophiles, and repeat offenders. The correctional facilities in the United States house many of these individuals.

It is also important to realize that they often present cool, calm, and in control when first confronted by law enforcement officers. This is a deception. The intent is to appear innocent. This is the calm before the storm. As long as a responding officer agrees with the person with this type of personality disorder, they usually remain calm and not threatening. As soon as individuals with this disorder feel they have the upper hand is when they are most dangerous. Remember, a suspect that is calm and relaxed is not necessarily a lower risk to you. I'd rather de-escalate a person who looks in emotional distress as opposed to one who is cool, calm, and collected! It is believed that there are two unofficial types of this disorder. You will not find much literature on the two types, but every law enforcement officer knows the difference. The hit-and-run type is the criminal who is not sophisticated in planning or committing crimes. They are often violent, angry, and overly controlling in relationships. They often commit impulsive crimes with minimal planning, and they are usually caught rather easily by police. It is also common for these individuals to be in repeated bar fights, commit sexual assaults, and have long criminal records. They also typically have a low criminal IQ. The kiss-and-suck unofficial subtype can be charming, engaging, and highly organized. They can disguise their true intent and often fool their victims. Ted Bundy, the serial killer, lured his victims into his van with his charm and good looks. He used crutches to deceive his victims into believing he needed assistance. When they offered a hand, he pushed them into the van and committed his crimes. His high intelligence helped him managed to evade police for years. The BTK killer had a family and home life and was considered a good citizen during the day. At night he became a cold-blooded killer. He also was highly organized and secretive in committing his crimes. Both were evil men with high intelligence. While they committed heinous crimes, which to the general public seemed crazy, both Bundy and BTK were not psychotic. There was no evidence of delusions, any hallucinations, or bizarre behavior evident. While the violent crimes committed by these two men and by other serial killers are hard to understand for most, this type of violent offender, while clearly sociopathic, is also known as a sexual sadist. A sexual sadist experiences pleasure when he or she is causing physical harm to others. Normal sexual relations do nothing or are not enough to feed these people's sadistic thoughts/fantasies.

There is no rehabilitation or medication available today to treat the sociopathic criminal. They cannot change unless they are committed to changing the way they think about others, and the most of these people are incapable of making this change.

## Narcissistic Personality Disorder

Narcissistic personality disorder is a disorder of personality seen in individuals who have inflated self-esteem. These individuals oftentimes feel they are superior in intellect, physical abilities, morality, and looks as compared to other people. In other words, they are "legends in their own minds." They are also not receptive to the ideas of others, which make them very difficult to get along with in relationships and in the workplace. Their romantic relationships are usually strained, as they are often described as being cold and unemotional. They are usually never satisfied with their partners and are always looking for someone smarter, more attractive, or more appealing than the people they are involved with. They also have an active fantasy life, dreaming of great riches, achievements, and conquest.

Chris Dormer, the ex-police officer who in 2013 shot and killed four, two of which were police officers, had many of the characteristics of narcissistic personality disorder. His manifesto, which he posted on his Facebook page, was the writings of an angry and vengeful man. There appeared little evidence in his writing that he was psychotic or was suffering from a major psychiatric disorder like schizophrenia. His writings were well organized and free of the bizarre beliefs or delusional content that would be expected in the writings of an individual with psychosis.

Dormer may have, like others with personality disorders, experience difficulty accepting criticism and handling loses, which may have set the stage for his murderous rage. It is also believed that underlying self-esteem issues can be one of the reasons individuals with this disorder have difficulty coping with or bouncing back from adversity. While this person presents as self-assured and confident on the outside, the narcissist usually has feelings of inadequacy and low self-worth on the inside. In Dormer's case, the firing appeared to be perceived as a direct personal attack on his name and reputation, which in his mind justified the killings. Consider his statements. "This is a necessary evil to force change in the LAPD." "I have exhausted all available means." "This was a last resort." These are phrases that to him justify his actions. His lack of empathy for others, another trait of narcissism, was evident by him taking the lives of civilians and police officers whom he had never met. Not taking responsibility for one's actions is another trait seen in both antisocial and narcissistic personality disorders. Statements in his manifesto such as "I lost my relationships with my mother and sister because of the LAPD" shows his inability to be responsible for his actions. Grandiosity (non-psychotic) and self-loathing is a key feature in this disorder. Going back to his manifesto statements, including "I had top-secret military clearance," "Journalist, I want you to investigate every location I resided in," "I am here to make change and make policy," "I am the reason TAC alert was established," and "Mrs. Obama, I love your new bangs," are examples of this grandiose trait.

So while Dormer appeared to have many of the traits of a narcissist, the question remains whether or not he was also suffering from a form of mental illness or brain injury. Is it possible that Dormer was depressed? Individuals who commit suicide are typically suffering from depression. His manifesto could be viewed by some as a sophisticated suicide note from a man expressing the feelings of hopelessness and despair seen in major depressive disorders. He used phrases such as "I have nothing to lose," "I do not fear death," and "I died a long time ago," which lead one to believe that a suicide-by-cop scenario might have occurred. He also said good-bye to many friends and wanted his brain to be preserved for research to study the effects of severe depression and repeated concussions, which he reported experiencing since 2008. The concussion reference may also be important, as studies show that individuals who sustain multiple concussions or other head injuries are at higher risk for depression and suicide. Former NFL star Junior Seau, who sustained multiple concussions over his playing career, was known by family, colleagues, and friends as a highly motivated person with a big heart and wide smile. On May 2, 2012, three years after he had retired from the NFL, Seau was found dead in his apartment with a self-inflicted gunshot wound. It appears that he may have been suffering in silence, not letting on to his family and friends about the severity of his emotional distress and deepening depression. Experts in the field believe that repeated blows to the head may damage a part of the brain called the frontal lobe. The frontal lobe, located just above our eyes, is responsible for giving us judgment, decision making, and impulse control. We believe that damage to this key area of the brain may cause a person to become more violent and aggressive toward self and/or others and may also cause difficulty making good decisions. This may explain the impulsive nature of Junior Seau's suicide as well as the impulsive killings and apparent suicide of ex-LAPD officer Chris Dormer. Getting back to the Dormer case, law enforcement authorities did hear a single gunshot before his cabin was engulfed in flames, leading one to believe that Dormer may have shot himself as police were closing in.

# CHAPTER 12

# SUBSTANCE ABUSE

Having to respond to calls involving intoxicated individuals has unfortunately become routine for many law enforcement officers. Calls involving bar fights, family disputes, domestic violence, sexual assault, and robbery often involve intoxicated individuals. While individuals who commit violent crimes should clearly be held accountable for their actions, alcohol, and illicit drugs play a big role in precipitating violent crime. Before we proceed in discussing how to manage these individuals when they are drunk, high, or unruly, it is important to first gain an understanding of why individuals get addicted to drugs and alcohol in the first place. While developing a better understanding of how to recognize and deal with intoxicated individuals is the purpose of this chapter, having a better understanding of substance abuse can also apply in an officer's personal life. It is well known that there are high rates of substance abuse in the law enforcement profession. It is not uncommon for my team to receive a call involving an off-duty officer involved in a domestic or community altercation because of substance abuse. It is also common for officers to assist family members, friends, and colleagues struggling with substance abuse issues get professional assistance when needed.

There are areas or circuits of the brain that are responsible for giving us feelings of pleasure. These pleasure circuits are located in one area of the brain known as the limbic system. The limbic system is a set of structures located deep within the brain that are believed to be the center of emotional expression. For example, emotions of rage, anger, happiness, and love all generate from brain regions located within our limbic system. This system is also responsible for keeping us safe by alerting us to dangerous situations within our environment. It helps us respond to threats and danger by directing us to either fight or flee from the situation. It directs survival behaviors, telling us to seek out food, water, sex, affection, and pleasure.

Also located within the limbic system is a special center or pathway that is responsible for giving us the experience of pleasure. This pathway is called the reward pathway, also known as the pleasure center. When we experience a pleasurable occurrence for the first time, such as eating ice cream, hitting a home run, achieving sexual orgasm, or receiving your first kiss, experts believe that dopamine, which is a brain chemical, is released within the reward pathway, thereby giving us feelings of pleasure. The reward pathway is programmed to identify pleasurable activities and to remind us to repeat the activity if we desire to experience pleasure or stress relief. The pleasurable activity is also strongly engraved into memory. For example, when we engage in pleasurable activities, our brains send direct signals to the reward pathway, telling it to create memories of the experience. Dopamine, one of the brains pleasure chemicals, is also being released at this time, giving us the feeling of pleasure. Our brains quickly make the connection between the pleasurable activity and dopamine release. The brain neatly files away the memory of the experience in nerve cells organized similar to documents in an office filing cabinet. These files hold our thoughts and memories of each pleasurable experience worthy of remembrance.

It usually takes a while for our pleasure circuits to "warm up to" or crave a pleasurable experience. Take the example of falling in love. Most folks do not fall in love at first sight. It takes a time to get to know a person before one's brain circuits light up with pleasure each time you see him or her. Over time the brain begins to crave the company of this person, as it remembers being rewarded with dopamine each time you are together. This same chemical process occurs for other enjoyable activities, such as yoga, biking, martial arts, painting, horseback riding, etc. As in falling in love, it takes a while for the brain to associate the activity with dopamine release and pleasure. But you can rest assured that once it makes the connection, you will be hooked!

Unlike the previous examples of pleasure circuits needing to warm up before they learn to crave an activity, drugs of abuse work a bit differently in the brain. For example, when heroin is injected into the body, it quickly enters the bloodstream at warp speed. Once in the blood, the drug rapidly enters the person's reward center, causing a jolt of intense pleasure. What makes drugs and alcohol so addicting are both the speed at which they reach the pleasure circuits and how much dopamine is released once they arrive there. It's believed that drugs of abuse highly excite the pleasure circuits, enhancing the amount of dopamine released. The more dopamine released, the more pleasure experienced by the user. Using cocaine as an example, when someone snorts cocaine, it quickly (within seconds) reaches the pleasure circuits. Once the drug arrives, it causes nerves in the pleasure circuits to release massive amounts of dopamine in the brain. This causes the rapid feeling of euphoria or high that the person experiences. The brain quickly files away the memory of this experience as being unique and highly pleasurable.

No other pleasurable experience (i.e., food, exercise, sex, etc.) compares with the intensity of this experience or produces more dopamine release in the brain. The brain enjoys this experience and tells the person to repeat the drug use over and over again. This leads to the rapid and destructive course of addiction. Eventually the brain craves both the massive discharge of dopamine caused by the drug and the pleasurable experience that follows. This is why a person addicted to drugs or alcohol will chose drug use over their family, job, relationships, etc. Normal life experiences no longer produce pleasure for the person. The only way these people can now experience pleasure is through drug use. This is why addiction is now classified as a brain disease.

During the past thirty years I've seen a good number of individuals, including law enforcement officers and military veterans, unable to resist these powerful cravings.

Remember, individuals addicted to alcohol or drugs are not craving the drug itself, but rather their brains are craving the pleasurable rush of dopamine they experience after each use. The brain is literally hijacked by the abused substance. If an individual's brain were not addicted to this chemical rush of pleasure, he or she would most likely see the error of these ways. This is why will power has nothing to do with ceasing drug use. Chemically addicted individuals are held hostage by the substances they abuse. Their brains are eventually tricked into believing that the drug is needed for survival. The drug-addicted individuals see their drug use as important as any basic human need.

You may be wondering why is it that some people become addicted and others do not. It's believed that some individuals may have what's been called supersensitive pleasure centers. In other words, their brains are highly sensitive to alcohol or drugs. Research now tells us that some individuals, because of genetics and family history, have a predisposition or greater chance of developing a substance abuse problem than the general population. To explain this further, let's take the example of two individuals who decide to stop at a local bar for drinks. As both men begin drinking their first beers, the first individual, whose brain is not addicted to alcohol, experiences a small rush of pleasure, as dopamine is released into his reward pathway. This dopamine release, which produces a calming effect, is not enough to hijack or convince his brain that drinking is needed for survival. The reward pathway of this person is not overly sensitive to substances of abuse. Individuals predisposed to alcohol or drug abuse have higher rates of developing a substance abuse disorder than the general population. Researchers still do not know why some individuals are extremely sensitive to drugs of abuse and others are not. Getting back to our example, the first person remembers that he needs to pick up his son at baseball practice and leaves the bar after he drinks only one beer. The second individual, who is genetically predisposed to alcohol (his father being an alcoholic), quickly downs his first beer and experiences a greater discharge of dopamine in his brain. His pleasure circuits light up like the strings on a Christmas tree, telling him to repeat the experience. Person two, after he downs his third drink and feels the strong urge to void, makes his way to the bathroom. On his way back from the bathroom he bumps into another patron, and without thinking, he starts a fight by throwing a punch.

It's also believed that some individuals addicted to alcohol or drugs may possibly have what is termed a reward deficiency syndrome. For some unexplained reason, pleasure circuits in some individuals do not light up and release dopamine for normal pleasures, such as sex, companionship, exercise, sports, and hobbies. Individuals with reward deficiency seek thrill and excitement through engaging in high-risk activities, such as gambling, drug use, heavy drinking, and fighting. Engaging in these activities turns on dopamine release and pleasure. Most of us repeat activities that bring us the feelings of pleasure. The problem for reward-deficient individuals is that they repeat activities that, while pleasurable, are destructive to both their physical and emotional health.

Alcohol and drug use shuts down a very important part of our brain called the prefrontal cortex (PFC), also known as our thinking brain. The PFC, which is located in the front part of our brains, is responsible for guiding our judgment, our impulse control, and our ability to make rational decisions when we are faced with challenging situations. This explains why people act inappropriately or say things out of character when they are under the influence of addictive substances. A person's ability to make decisions and understand the consequences of his or her actions is impaired by drugs and alcohol, which explains why we see such high rates of violence in people who are intoxicated.

It is now believed that having a family history of alcohol abuse, and pleasure-center abnormalities are at the root of substance abuse problems. Can pleasure circuits ever return back to normal?

Unfortunately it appears that these pleasure circuits never can return to normal in relation to substance use. This is why people addicted to alcohol or drugs can never again use their drug of choice. It only takes one drink or one use of Illicit drugs to again excite and light up their pleasure circuits, reinforcing the desire or craving to repeat the substance use experience. Their brains will always light up, releasing large amounts of dopamine each time they use. This is called relapse. Relapse will occur each time a person drinks or uses drugs. It's known that even reminders of substance use experiences (called triggers) can set off relapses. Examples of triggers are sensory reminders of abuse, such as smelling a cigar, walking by a bar, or bumping into old drinking buddies. These experiences can excite the brain by releasing small amounts of dopamine, giving the individual a strong urge or craving to seek out alcohol or drugs. And while pleasure centers will always remain sensitive to the person's drug of choice, the good news is that the individual's pleasure circuits should slowly begin to adjust back to normal for nonsubstance-related pleasures once he or she is free of substances. When people first begin treatment and are free of substances in their systems, it is not uncommon for them to feel sick, weak, dizzy, emotionally numb, and irritable. These physical symptoms can be expected, as the individual's nervous system is trying to function without the drug. This is called withdrawal. Think of withdrawal as nerves within the nervous system becoming more and more irritable as each hour goes by without the drug.

Withdrawal is usually treated at an inpatient detoxification treatment facility. In the case of alcohol, detoxifying drugs that are cross-tolerant to alcohol (similar to the action of alcohol), such as minor tranquilizers or antiseizure medication, are prescribed and slowly withdrawn during a three- to five-day period. This treatment allows the brain and body to slowly begin to function again as the tranquilizer dose is decreased each day. Upon completion of an alcohol or drug detoxification treatment program, the individual must enter an outpatient program. In most outpatient programs the individual receives treatment in an office setting and is allowed to go home at night. A residential program is a twenty-four-hour, supervised setting where the individual lives until the completion of treatment. The old adage "If you first don't succeed, try, try again" is very pertinent to substance abuse treatment. It is not uncommon for a person to experience multiple failed attempts at quitting before he or she is successful. An effective treatment program should include individual, family, and group treatment options. The treatment program should also have access to a psychiatrist in case medications are needed to treat withdrawal, depression, anxiety, or PTSD.

Drugs commonly abused by individuals suffering from an anxiety disorder (PTSD) or depression are alcohol and /or painkillers known as narcotics. Both alcohol and narcotics, such as heroin and prescribed pain relievers, relieve the intrusive thoughts, irritability, hypervigilance, and insomnia seen in most of these psychiatric disorders. Underlying psychiatric disorders are fairly common in individuals suffering from substance use disorders. Psychiatric disorders are not usually diagnosed until two weeks after detoxification, as individuals are expected to experience emotional and physical difficulty while they are withdrawing from alcohol or drugs. It is usually at the conclusion of withdrawal that the individual with either major depression or an anxiety disorder would begin to experience the disabling symptoms of these disorders. For many, alcohol and illicit drugs served as a way to self-medicate the feeling of anxiety or depression. Alcohol and drugs can cause temporary relief from these disorders by relaxing the nervous system and making it easier for the individual to function. The problem with self-medicating these disorders with drugs or alcohol is that the effect of the substance is short-lived. Therefore, the person's symptoms soon return, reinforcing the need to take the drug. Drugs of abuse also take their toll on the physical health of the addicted individual. Studies also show higher rates of high blood pressure, high cholesterol, ulcers, and strokes in individuals diagnosed with substance use disorders.

One of the major goals of substance abuse treatment is to restore normal pleasure center function. This is accomplished by having the individual reexperience nonsubstance-related pleasurable activities. The individual's pleasure circuits are in need of a readjustment or reprogramming once the person is substance-free. While the individuals' pleasure centers will always remain sensitive to their drug of choice, exposing them to nonsubstance-related activities and events will hopefully reset these pleasure circuits back to normal. This should allow them to again enjoy family relationships as well as other enjoyable nonsubstance-related activities.

Today there are a host of new medicines that help relieve both withdrawal symptoms and the craving experienced with drug use. Using medication to assist a person in stopping alcohol and drug use is called medication-assisted treatment. For example, medications such as Naltrexone, Vivatrol, and Campral can help reduce the powerful cravings experienced in alcohol abuse. New medications are also available to treat heroin and/or other narcotic addictions. Narcotics are also known as painkillers. Abuse of prescribed and nonprescribed painkillers, such as Vicodin, Percocet, and Oxycontin, are on the rise is the United States. Alarmingly recent studies also show that abuse of painkillers are on the rise in the eighteen-to-twenty-five age groups here in the United States as well as in veterans returning from Iraq and Afghanistan. What make these drugs so popular are their abilities to produce tranquility, sedation, pain relief, and relaxation. When individuals addicted to painkillers attempt to stop using, they experience both a physical withdrawal and intense craving to keep taking the drug. While medications like methadone have been available for years to treat narcotic addiction, newer medications, such as buprenorphine, are now available. Buprenorphine is now available in two forms—Suboxone and Subutex. Buprenorphine acts by quickly stopping the uncomfortable withdrawal and cravings during a three- to seven-day period. This quick response makes for a more successful recovery. Suboxone contains a second drug called Naloxone to help deter misuse. If a tablet of Suboxone is crushed and injected, a common practice by abusers of painkillers, the Naloxone will cause the person to get physically sick. Naloxone is a type of medication insurance policy against the misuse of Suboxone. Both formulations can now be prescribed in outpatient office settings. Only physicians certified to prescribe Suboxone are allowed to initiate treatment on an outpatient basis. This means that a person wanting to seek treatment with medication for painkiller or narcotic addiction can now be treated in a private physician's office as opposed to the past practice of one either going to a methadone clinic or being admitted to a hospital-based treatment facility.

Alcohol and/or illicit drugs effectively shut down the part of the brain responsible for giving a person judgment and rational thought. This removal of judgment and rational thought is the main reason intoxicated individuals are unpredictable, easily agitated, and physically aggressive and will say and act counter to their sober beliefs. We also know that intoxicated individuals are more likely to be involved in violent encounters with police. A study conducted by Lt. James McElvain of the Riverside County Sheriff's Department and titled "Shot's Fired: An Examination in of Police Shootings and Citizen Behaviors" revealed that those under the influence of drugs were three times more likely during an encounter to be shot or shot at by officers than individuals who were not intoxicated, according to the study. The study, which reviewed five years of the sheriff's department data regarding police shootings, revealed that about 70 percent of the civilians involved in officer shootings were under some kind of chemical influence (PoliceOne.com, and the Force Science Institute, 2/12/2007).

There is a general rule of thumb when one is dealing with an intoxicated individual. Expect the unexpected! People under the influence, whether encountered during traffic stops or in a community setting, oftentimes represent threats to themselves, others, and the officers involved. These situations present many challenges for the officers involved. Officers need to rapidly assess the capabilities and intent of the individual while they simultaneously rely on verbal skills to gain compliance. While using verbal de-escalation techniques is the preferred technique for dealing with nonviolent, intoxicated individuals, these situations can become volatile and dangerous rather quickly, requiring officers to utilize less lethal and other options to ensure their safety as well as the safety of the community. In the field, experience and time on the job can become an officer's greatest ally when one is interacting with an intoxicated individual. Most veteran officers have learned through experience that these calls can be deadly if not taken seriously.

## Common Drugs of Abuse

### Narcotics (Heroin, Morphine, Vicodin, Oxycontin, Methadone, Demerol)

**Action:** Narcotics are known to causes sedation, pain relief, and respiratory depression if taken in larger amounts. It is believed that narcotic drugs, such as heroin, slow down brain activity including brain areas responsible for movement, emotion, breathing and thought processes. A person under the influence of narcotics will appear with *pinpoint pupils* (small); may be euphoric, overly drowsiness or unconscious. Injection sites (needle marks) may be evident. If narcotic overdose is suspected, (shallow breathing and unconscious), the medication Narcan is administered, available in injection or nasal spray form. While historically Narcan is administered by rescue personnel, police officers in several states are now being trained in administrating this drug prior to the arrival of rescue as the quicker the drug gets into the system the greater chance of survival. The good news is that this drug is very safe and can not cause complications if given to someone who is not overdosing – you can breath a sigh of relief!

**Withdrawal:** Withdrawal symptoms include runny nose, muscle spasms, vomiting, watery eyes, *large pupils*, yawning, sweats, and diarrhea.

# Stimulants (Cocaine, Methamphetamine, Amphetamine)

**Action:** As covered earlier, stimulants speed up brain circuits and have been known to cause euphoria, increased excitement, increased blood pressure, insomnia, and *large pupils*. Stimulants can also cause *excited delirium*, psychosis, violence, aggression, agitation, and increased strength.

**Withdrawal:** Withdrawal from stimulants is usually not life threatening. The person may experience depression, apathy, increased sleep, and irritability.

**Overdose:** Stimulant overdose can be serious, and has been known to cause high blood pressure, seizures and cardiac arrest

# Depressants (Alcohol, Valium, Xanax, Ativan, Klonopin)

**Action:** All depressants slow down brain functioning. Depressants may cause sedation, unsteady gait, slurred speech, large pupils and confusion. Overdose can cause dilated (big) pupils, shallow breathing, clammy skin, weak and rapid pulse, seizures, and death. This is one class of medication that can cause serious medical complications during detoxification. Most individuals trying to quit will need some form of medical detox.

**Withdrawal:** Withdrawal symptoms include anxiety, irritability, seizures, tremors, upset stomach, vomiting and high blood pressure. While in detoxification individuals are given medication similar to the action of the drug, such as Librium or Phenobarbital, which enhances a safe and non-complicated withdrawal.

# Hallucinogens (PCP, Marijuana, LSD, Ecstasy)

**Action**: All hallucinogens are known to cause a state of euphoria. individuals can also experience hallucinations, fatigue, paranoia, psychosis, muscle weakness, dilated (big) pupils, increased appetite, profuse sweating (ecstasy, PCP). As stated earlier, *excited delirium* can occur.

**Withdrawal**: Withdrawal symptoms include Insomnia, depression, anxiety, and are not usually life threatening.

# Other (Bath Salts and Inhalants)

**Action**: Bath salts are known excite the brain and often cause psychosis, agitation, aggression, *excited delirium, large pupils*, and increased strength. Withdrawal symptoms may be similar to that seen in stimulants. **Inhalants** are a class of substances that (paint, gas, lighter fluid) can resemble alcohol intoxication. Inhalants are highly toxic to the brain. There is no detoxification required for inhalant abuse.

Earlier we discussed the importance of knowing a person's past history of violent behaviors before getting to the scene. While this is not often possible, the more you know about a person, the better prepared you will be. The good news is that all of the interventions suggested in chapter 1 on excited delirium are applicable when one is dealing with an intoxicated suspect. The following tips are also helpful when you are dealing with an intoxicated suspect:

+ Just as in working with a person suffering from mental illness, these situations need time to resolve. Rushing in quickly to go hands-on oftentimes escalates violence. As long as the intoxicated person is not assaulting others or engaging in self-harm, you have time!

- All dispatch personnel should receive training in mental illness, substance awareness, and excited delirium. Providing training to dispatch personnel should improve proficiencies in history taking, information gathering, and identifying problematic behaviors.

- A naked or disrobing person is usually under the influence of substances or is psychotic. This is a very common presentation in excited delirium. Never approach a person with this presentation alone!

- Intoxicated individuals, as with psychosis and excited delirium, may not respond to OC spray. OC spray tends to increase agitation and aggression in some intoxicated individuals.

- Individuals high on cocaine, amphetamines, PCP, and bath salts may oftentime have excessive strength. This is one of the main reasons to wait for backup in these cases. Substance intoxication with stimulants can excessively increase adrenalin levels, which translate into increased aggression and power.

- Intoxicated individuals may be impervious to pain and at risk for both hypothermia (frostbite) and hyperthermia (excessive sweating). This is why other less lethal options such as the baton or self-defense techniques may be ineffective. Heavily intoxicated individuals are also at risk for breathing difficulties secondary to vomiting and asphyxiation (restraint). This is why having rescue staged in the area is a good idea. This level of substance intoxication needs to be viewed as a medical emergency.

- Never restrain alone! If you understand the safety concerns as mentioned above, that's enough said!

+ The Taser has been helpful in these situations. Have it on hand or call for it to be brought to the scene. As stated earlier, once suspects are tased, sit them up or place on their sides to prevent respiratory arrest.

+ One officer should do the talking. An intoxicated individual may have trouble focusing and concentrating. Focusing on one voice is easier than trying to focus on multiple speakers. It is also important to limit side conversations, as the person may interpret these conversations as ones involving him or her.

+ Remember to keep a safe distance. Do not compromise safety for rapport. The intoxicated individual is most often uncooperative, impulsive, and unpredictable. He or she may also misinterpret your closeness as an attack. Do not touch the individual unless going hands-on, as this may precipitate a violent reaction. If an intoxicated person bumps into you, easily guide him or her away. Do not physically restrain unless the person is posing a threat to you or others.

+ As for a mentally ill suspect, try to limit noise, sirens, and chaos at the scene. It is much easier for a person who is intoxicated to concentrate if background noise is reduced.

+ Use a neutral tone of voice. Do not raise your voice unless the person is not responding to your neutral tone .Do not yell back, make fun of, or say hurtful things. This approach oftentimes leads to a violent counter, as the intoxicated person is quick to go into fight mode.

+ If possible, tell the person what you are going to do before you do it. Making quick and abrupt moves can startle both a psychotic and intoxicated individual into physical aggression as a self-protective action. Remember, the person may misperceive your intentions, so be clear and concise in your communication. Give one direction at a time instead of giving multiple instructions all at once. "John, I will walk with you to the ambulance. I'm going to help you stand."

+ Give clear instructions and repeat yourself until the person looks at you and responds. You can say, "Sir, I need you to sit down before I can figure out how to help you." Getting an intoxicated person to sit down gives you valuable information regarding the person's willingness to comply with your directives. Offering structure and direction also helps the person regain the feeling of being in control.

+ For the intoxicated person who is rambling, try to listen and show concern. "Hey, I would be upset too if that happened." Use understanding body postures, such as nodding, as the person speaks. Again, when you are using verbal skills, remain vigilant, as intoxicated individuals can become aggressive quickly.

+ Remember to continue to practice good officer safety when you are escorting an intoxicated individual into a rescue. Check all pockets as you would any other suspect, as the person may have a concealed weapon. Officers have been killed in the line of duty for not taking the intoxicated individual seriously.

+ Time is on your side as long as the person is not violent. Oftentimes with a little patience and understanding an intoxicated individual will eventually comply with your directives.

+ Remember, treat substance intoxication as you would a medical problem, or it could end badly for all involved.

# CHAPTER 13

# NEURODEVELOPMENTAL DISABILITIES

A child or adult with a neurodevelopmental disability is not suffering from mental illness. While there may be some similarities in presentation, there are many key differences. While it is not the job of law enforcement to diagnosis, understanding the difference between someone with a developmental disorder like autism and someone with a mental illness like schizophrenia can help achieve a successful intervention. One key difference between the two is that neurodevelopmental disorders are most often first noticed in early childhood as opposed to mental illness, which usually develops in one's late teens or early twenties.

A developmental disability is usually suspected when a child fails to meet expected milestones, such as saying his or her first words, smiling, pointing, or taking his or her first steps. Parents may also notice their children may seem to lack social skills (plays alone) or fails to bond physically or emotionally with parents and siblings (doesn't like to be held). A child with an intellectual disability, formally known as mental retardation, will have a noticeable deficiency in intelligence (low IQ), learning, use of language, and motor skills (feeding, walking, dressing, etc.). So while language, learning, and communication difficulties are prominent in a child with an intellectual disability, behavioral abnormalities, such as biting, kicking, and head banging, may also be seen. As is the case with many types of disorders, there are different levels of severity in individuals diagnosed with developmental disabilities.

Autism is a disorder that also is first evident in early childhood. There are also different levels of severity for autism from low- to high-functioning. Children and adults with autism have difficulty understanding social cues and appear awkward and uncomfortable in social situations. They may appear overly sensitive or misinterpret what is said to them. It is also common for individuals with autism to have heightened senses, particularly with hearing and touch. Being overly focused on repetitive play and having difficulty changing routines is also common. They may eat the same foods every day and have strict routines, and they may be intolerant of any changes in daily activities. One characteristic that is different in autism is that intelligence may not be affected. Some Individuals with autism are highly intelligent. They are at times seen as being nerdy, highly intelligent but socially awkward. In the hit TV sitcom *The Big Bang Theory* (CBS), the character Sheldon plays a scientist with classic features of adult autism. He needs to sit in the same section of the couch and eat the same foods. He is overly focused in superhero comics/video games. He dresses the same each day and lives his life by strict rules and routines. As many with autism, he can experience extreme anxiety if any of these routines are interfered with. It is common for individuals with autism to also suffer with simultaneously occurring psychiatric disorders, such as anxiety, depression, and obsessive compulsive disorder.

The good news is that many of the crisis intervention techniques used for mentally ill individuals in crisis can be effective in de-escalating an adolescent or adult with autism. While parents are usually able to safely manage the behavior difficulties with autistic children, because of their size and strength, adolescents and young adults can become very difficult to manage without assistance being provided by multiple family members, behavioral specialists, or local police. While no parent wants to place that 911 call, sometimes it is the only short-term solution. While adolescence is a difficult transition for most, the autistic teen may experience this transition with more anxiety, frustration, fear, and uncertainty, as relationships become more complex (making friends) and improved socialization with others and in the classroom is needed. Remember, most autistic teens have difficulty communicating their thoughts and feeling and also have great difficulty picking up social cues (will misread sarcasm) in conversation. Not having these skills may precipitate a crisis.

The following techniques have been found to be helpful when one is faced with a highly agitated teen or adult with autism of other developmental disabilities:

- Remember, many autistic individuals are oversensitive to external stimuli, such as sounds, smells, and touch, as is someone who is in a crisis because of mental illness. By staying calm and reducing field chaos (sirens and distractions), a responding officer can enhance the individual's ability to focus on his or her words and instructions.
- Keep communication very specific. Talking slowly and using one to two words at a time can make it easier for the individual to follow your lead.
- Use normalization skills. You can say, "I can see you're upset. If that had happened to me, I'd be upset too. I am here to help you today." These statements all convey an attempt to understand the individual.

- Help these individuals understand that you will help them stay in control and that you are not going to let anyone get hurt today.

- Walk or pace with the individual or go to a quiet place to limit distractions.

- Try to remove individuals who appear to be escalating the situation. This could include parents, friends, employers, etc.

- Remember, autistic individuals have difficulty with change and loss. A death in the family, loss of job, and change in school/classroom may precipitate a crisis.

- Demonstrate what you want them to do. This could involve helping them with breathing, having them walk with you to a quiet area, or demonstrating how you want them to put down objects they are holding.

- Remember, yelling, screaming, rocking, or walking may be their attempt to communicate their thoughts and feelings. These can be self-soothing behaviors that you can allow to continue as long as they are not physically violent.

- Always remember to continue to practice officer safety skills during these interventions, as some autistic teens and adults can become physically violent and require restraint. The Taser could be deployed in these situations for safety.

- Using diversionary tactics like asking questions about one of their hobbies or interests may help lower anxiety levels in some cases.

# CHAPTER 14

# GUN VIOLENCE AND MENTAL ILLNESS—WHAT NEXT?

It is very important to remember that it is not a diagnosis that makes an individual dangerous. It is person's history of violence that determines future risk. Gavin De Becker, one of the nation's leading experts in predicting violent behavior, published a book titled *The Gift of Fear*. In his book, De Becker points out that as human beings many of us have the ability to predict violence. We may not know how or when, but we may be able to tell which individuals are at risk to commit violent crimes by using our survival intuition. De Becker teaches in his book that in the human brain we have a built-in alarm system called the amygdala. When the amygdala picks up a potential threat, it sends us warning signals, such as the feelings of fear, apprehension, doubt, and suspicion, which guide us away from danger. If we discount these feeling, we oftentimes put ourselves in great danger. We have all heard or read of cases where individuals, after violent events occur, will oftentimes tell police that they knew something was going on with the perpetrators or were scared that something was about to happen. This premonition is a common survival signal sent out by the amygdala that must not be ignored! Men call this survival signal their gut, while women call it intuition. Paying attention to one's intuition is key to staying safe, which is the premise of Gavin de Becker's book.

So if a mentally ill individual has a history of becoming physically violent when in crisis, there is a greater likelihood of violence occurring again in the future. It is important to again keep in mind that the majority of violent acts committed in the United States are perpetrated by offenders who are not mentally ill. This is also true of gun violence. The majority of homicides in the world are committed by individuals who are not mentally ill. The majority of violent assaults, rapes, gang violence, terrorist attacks, shootings, and child abuse are also committed by adults who are not mentally ill. In other words, the majority of these individuals knew the consequences of their actions, had motives, were organized in planning their actions, and attempted to evade law enforcement. They also, for the most part, were free of psychosis and/or symptoms of other major psychiatric disorders, such as bipolar disorder.

A clear example is the Boston bombing in 2013. From all accounts, both perpetrators were organized, had motive (justified in their own minds), knew the consequences of their actions, and lacked empathy for their victims. These characteristics are more consistent with antisocial personality disorder (the sociopath) than a major mental illness. So why is there such a strong debate over whether or not mentally ill individuals should have access to guns? As we already said, the majority do not commit felony assaults or homicides using firearms.

Unfortunately the cases previously discussed, such as Virginia Tech, Aurora, the US Capitol shootings, Newtown, and the Washington Navy Shipyard shooting, were all mass shootings involving individuals with untreated mental illness. So while the percentages are very low, mentally ill adults can commit violent acts when certain factors are present, including the following:

+ not receiving or taking prescribed medications
+ a history of violence toward others
+ access to firearms
+ delusional beliefs that others are plotting, trying to kill, or spreading rumors about them
+ experiencing command hallucinations that tell them to harm others
+ increased use of illicit substances
+ increased depression with expressed hopelessness, despair, and inappropriate guilt.
+ giving away prized possessions, acting out of character, quitting their jobs, or making statements about righting some perceived injustice
+ escalating violent acts like breaking or throwing objects, discharging firearms in public, or wielding bladed weapons
+ engaging in violent/graphic writing involving blood, shooting, stabbing, or mass carnage toward others

Any of the above behaviors may be considered early warning signs of an impending safety issue for the individual or the officers involved. If a person with several of the previously mentioned risk factors has or is in the process of accessing a firearm and no emergency intervention takes place, it's just a matter of time before something bad happens.

Most of the mass killers mentioned in this book purchased their firearms and ammunition legally or stole/used weapons purchased by family members. They passed criminal background checks, as they were not identified as being convicted felons or illegal immigrants. The court did not determine that they were mentally ill or mentally defective, and they have not been committed to psychiatric facilities. Cho, the Virginia Tech shooter, despite being deemed mentally ill and a danger to self and others by the courts, passed federal background checks and was able to freely purchased firearms and ammunition. Clearly the Virginia Tech tragedy identified that there are issues with the criminal background check system. While the federal background system appears to identify convicted felons and illegal immigrants, it does not mandate states to release their mental health records. Holmes, the Aurora movie theater shooter, purchased his firearms legally, as he passed all background checks. He was not a felon, illegal alien, or adjudicated mentally defective. (I hate that term and only us it because it is the wording in the federal law!). Alexis, the navy shipyard shooter, also purchased his firearms legally and passed criminal background checks. Alexis's mental health records, like Cho's and Holmes's, were not accessed or confirmed by the background checks. The Newtown shooter did not purchase his firearms. They belonged to his mother, who had purchased them legally. Guns also need to be secured under lock and key. Several school shooters were able to access their parents' firearms with ease. One question is whether parents should be held legally responsible for the violent crimes committed by their children? This needs to be consided in the future.

Many countries like Australia and Great Britain have aggressively and successfully passed gun reform laws after mass shooting events in their countries. For example, after a mass shooting in Australia in 1996, the government quickly passed laws to ban personal ownership of assault weapons and shotguns, and made it more difficult for private citizen's to purchase guns through tougher licensing and background check reforms. The key here is the swift action of government officials to place partisanship politics aside to ensure public safety—something that is difficult to come by here in America.

Here in the United States, it is clear that making the purchase and distribution of semiautomatics, large-capacity magazines, and certain handguns illegal for private ownership along with many of the other tougher restrictions placed on gun ownership (already with great success in other countries) is a must. Hopefully our leaders can put aside partisanship politics and come to some agreement on this issue before more innocent Americans have to die by gun violence.

What role does the video gaming industry play in all of this? Video games that are violent and involve shooting, stabbing, or killing others should not be available to children and teens. I have seen far too many parents who either turn a blind eye to or are clueless on the negative impact these games have on developing young minds. Is it a coincidence that most of the teenage and young adult killers in the United States spent countless hours at home, racking up kills on these games? Excessive use of these games may be desensitizing vulnerable youths like Adam Lanza, the Newtown killer, to killing. There needs to be tighter restrictions on access and production of these violent games and more responsibility by parents in restricting their use.

When it comes to making mental health records available, there is a strong debate regarding the right to privacy, the right to bear arms, and gun control. Should states be required to make its mental health records available as part of gun owner purchase/background checks? Would this make a difference? While I think we need to tighten up this system, it is this writer's opinion that mental health records should be made available with restrictions. While my thoughts on this topic may not be popular within the mental health community, I believe that the following could be used as a guideline as to who would be restricted from purchasing firearms:

+ Individuals diagnosed with a psychotic disorder, or a major mood disorder such as bipolar disorder, with a history of involuntary hospitalization. .

- Individuals with diagnosed personality disorders who have a history of involuntary certification and multiple episodes of self-abuse and/or violence toward others.

- Individuals with repeated episodes of major depression with a history of hospitalizations for suicide attempts or violence toward others.

- Individuals with multiple involuntary hospitalizations to a mental health facility due to being a danger to self or others.

- Individuals with a chronic history of substance abuse who have repeated detoxification admissions or psychiatric hospitalizations. (The Brady Law does identify addiction as an issue that should restrict gun ownership.)

While stricter guidelines regarding gun ownership are needed, gun control alone is not the answer. Examining all facets of the problem, including a review of the involuntary commitment law, appears warranted. Another issue may be the mental health system itself. The current mental health system in many states is set up to treat individuals who voluntarily seek out help or accept mental health treatment. Individuals who refuse treatment, who go off their medication, or who are tortured by daily hallucinations and/or delusions do not typically seek out help. Oftentimes law enforcement officers are called by concerned family members, neighbors, or other concerned citizens who request assistance in regards to a psychotic individual acting out in the community. These individuals when in crisis don't often come in contact with mental health professionals until they are taken to the hospital by police. In fact, law enforcement officers have become the frontline mental health workers, not something they expected when they decided to enter a career in law enforcement. This is why it is critical for officers to learn de-escalation and crisis intervention skills. Many of the officers I've trained and work with have excellent communication skills and are better prepared to deal with a mental health crisis than a good number of mental health professionals. For example, who do social workers, psychiatric nurses, counselors, psychologist, and even psychiatrist call when mental health clients are presenting in tenuous control? They call police officers. Law enforcement officers are also better at assessing dangerousness than the majority of mental health professionals. Don't get me wrong. There are many highly skilled clinicians in the previously mentioned disciplines who are qualified to determine a person's risk of dangerousness. There just aren't enough to get the job done. State funding cuts to mental health organizations as well as the lack of specialized training for clinicians in determining risk appear to be part of the problem. Family members are oftentimes told by mental health staff that they need to wait until the person becomes violent or suicidal in order for clinicians to act. The mental health system needs to be proactive and not just reactive. Even with reduced recourses the mental health community needs to respond to this issue with new ideas, training, and interventions to assist law enforcement in addressing this serious problem. Increased training for law enforcement in the recognition of and response to the mentally ill needs to be part of annualized training programs. My home state of Rhode Island is no exception. After three deadly force incidents involving mentally ill individuals, I partnered with now retired police Lt. Robin Winslow to design the unique certification program called the certified crisis responder training or CCRT, which I mentioned in earlier chapters. This intensive four-day program, which includes eight hours of role-play scenarios, prepares officers on how to identify and respond to mentally ill individuals in crisis. Experienced role-players consisting of law enforcement officers and mental health professionals act out various crisis situations in a variety of settings, including baseball fields, parking lots, alleyways, school gymnasiums, and office settings. Officer participants are tested and scored on their abilities to communicate effectively, de-escalate the situation, give the situation time, and select appropriate use of force techniques. Officers also receive information on how to recognize the symptoms of mental illness, a review of use-of-force protocols, including proper restraint and Taser deployment, information on excited delirium, and crisis/de-escalation techniques. Officers are also trained in how to present this information to their department in order to ensure the sustainability of this information. My training team also provides a four-hour version of this program provided as part of annualized training for many police departments. The good news is that there has been a significant reduction in community incidents within our home state since the development of this and similar training programs for law enforcement. Similar programs like the CIT program, which was developed by the Albuquerque PD, pioneered the development of this type of programming for police. The Albuquerque program has served as a model for mental health training for police departments nationwide.

There also needs to be better coordination and consultation between mental health, education professionals, and law enforcement. Communities should explore the development of rapid-response and evaluation teams consisting of law enforcement, mental health professionals, and school social workers/administrators. These teams could possibly provide immediate assessment and seventy-two-hour holds on individuals found to be in imminent risk of committing violent acts. While the ACLU may argue about the legalities of this type of intervention, time is of the essence when we are dealing with these situations. Waiting for the violent or suicidal act to occur can no longer be the standard. A modification of the existing mental health and involuntary commitment law may need to occur to support the idea of rapid-response teams. It also may be a good idea to have armed officers or specialty trained security (military veterans and retired law enforcement officers) at all schools in the United States. We should follow the model of the Israelis, who have armed security at all schools in their country. When is the last time you heard of a school shooting in Israel? They simply do not occur. It may also be a good idea to provide education to the media and the general population on the early warning signs of violence; when and how to report concerns, as well as the importance of not overpublicizing these events.

So the outlined ideas should be considered as part of a comprehensive plan of response to the increase in mass violence incidents here in the United States as well as a tool to educate both law enforcement and the general public on the how to recognize and respond to a mental health crisis.

# AFTERWORD

Choosing to specialize in this training and consultation field has been rewarding. I made this decision around fifteen years ago after the completion of my first law enforcement training. Being a military veteran and understanding military culture gave me great insight into how to deliver my message. As a medic assigned to an infantry unit, I needed to be knowledgeable and confident in my medical abilities while I respected the very different expertise of the infantry soldiers (affectionately known as grunts) assigned to my company. I applied this principle of mutual respect in all law enforcement trainings with great success. Officers in attendance would learn from me, and I would learn from them. This partnership would prove successful in improving safety for officers responding to calls/incidents involving individuals experiencing mental health crises as well as the mentally ill individuals involved in these encounters. The Certified Crisis Responder Program, while successfully training officers in crisis techniques, has also produced many excellent police trainers. Certified police officers like Officer Richard Parenti from the Scituate Police Department, Sgt. Villiard from the Woonsocket Police Department, Police Chief Rick Ramsey from the West Greenwich Police Department, Officer Sandra Marinucci, and Sgt. Roland Coutu from the West Warwick PD, and retired police Lt. Robin Winslow from the Coventry Police Department were from the first class of CCRT officers certified in Rhode Island. All have been invaluable to the ongoing success of this program, volunteering countless hours to assist their fellow officers in understanding this very important officer training skill. CCRT officers have also participated in facilitating training segments of the three-day CCRT trainings and in providing smaller statewide department-based trainings when requested. Trained officers also volunteer their time to actively participate in role-play scenarios alongside mental health professionals as both role-players and evaluators. CCRT officers by far make the best role-players. They are able to take their learned knowledge of mental illness and act out scenarios, making the experience both challenging and reality-based for their fellow officers in attendance. I am also thankful for the training assistance (role-plays) provided by local mental health professionals in making this training program successful.

I am also thankful for the caring and compassion shown by our trained officers in responding to mentally ill individuals in crisis. Yes, I did say caring and compassion! While they are not out hugging trees, trained officers and most police officers in general enter their profession to help others. Like many civilians, officers have family members with mental illnesses or developmental disabilities like autism. This gives many officers hands-on experience at home, which translates to greater empathy in the field.